Palestine and the Anglo-American Connection, 1945–1950

American University Studies

Series IX
History

Vol. 17

PETER LANG
New York · Berne · Frankfurt am Main

Miriam Joyce Haron

Palestine and the Anglo-American Connection, 1945–1950

PETER LANG
New York · Berne · Frankfurt am Main

CIP-Kurztitelaufnahme der Deutschen Bibliothek

Haron, Miriam Joyce:
Palestine and the Anglo-American Connection,
1945–1950 / Miriam Joyce Haron. – New York;
Berne; Frankfurt am Main: Lang, 1986.
(American University Studies: Ser. 9,
History; Vol. 17)
ISBN 0-8204-0292-3

NE: American University Studies / 09

Library of Congress Catalog Card Number:
85-31234
ISBN 0-8204-0292-3
ISSN 0740-0462

© Peter Lang Publishing, Inc., New York 1986

Printed by Lang Druck Inc., Liebefeld/Berne (Switzerland)

For my sons

Joshua Victor Haron

and

Adam Ben Haron

TABLE OF CONTENTS

PREFACE

The Palestine question has received considerable attention
from scholars, but the Anglo-American aspect of the problem has
been neglected. Because both Britain and the United States took
leading roles in the disposition of Palestine after World War II
a study of Anglo-American involvement in the matter is important
background for an understanding of the complex issues surrounding
relations between Arabs and Jews, and at the same time sheds
light on tensions between Washington and London. I first used
the title Palestine And The Anglo-American Connection in a short
article published in Modern Judaism and then decided the topic
needed more attention.

This is a short book, but in writing it I have incurred a
large debt. I appreciate grants received from both the National
Endowment for the Humanities, and the Harry S. Truman Library.
I am especially grateful for assistance from Elizabeth Safley at
the Truman Library. Wherever the Palestine problem took me I
benefitted from the encouragement of Ruth and Solomon Bernards,
Lilian Derecktor, and the late Samuel Derecktor. In addition,
I was aided by the unfailing cooperation of David Haron.

Finally I wish to offer special thanks to my friend Robert
H. Ferrell who patiently read the manuscript and made useful
comments.

Miriam Joyce Haron

CHAPTER 1

INTRODUCTION

During the initial years after the Second World War the
United States and Great Britain generally followed similar
foreign policies, with the American government frequently in the
lead; but there was one area in which near-complete disagreement
took place, and that was the disposition of what then was known
as Palestine. Britain had emerged from the war exhausted and on
the verge of bankruptcy and it soon became clear that London
would no longer be able to maintain a position of leadership in
world affairs or even hold a remnant of the once mighty British
empire. The Americans were in a completely different position--
the war ended as the nuclear age began, and with a monopoly of
the atomic bomb the United States was the most powerful nation
on earth. Having finally understood the folly of isolationism
the American government also gave some evidence of willingness
to assume the role of superpower. After victory over the Axis
powers the Cold War followed. Wartime partnership was replaced
by opposition to the Soviet Union. Fear of Russian intentions
drew London and Washington into a working relationship, and
Palestine soon figured--discordantly, as it turned out--in this
relationship.

While involvement of the United States government in the
problem of Palestine was mainly a matter of the years immediately
after 1945, it is possible to trace what one might describe as
concern over Palestine back to the era of the First World War,

when the British government in 1917 found it expedient to make a
gesture toward the Zionist movement. Despite opposition from
the only Jewish member of the government, at that time, Edwin
Montagu, Secretary of State for India, who feared a Moslem
reaction, the foreign secretary of the Lloyd George Cabinet,
Arthur Balfour, sent a letter on November 2, 1917 to one of the
leading representatives of the Zionist cause in England, Lord
Walter Rothschild, expressing Britain's interest in establishment
of a Jewish national home in Palestine. This letter became known
as the Balfour Declaration. Before issuing that declaration
Balfour had visited Washington and in a conversation with Justice
Louis D. Brandeis of the Supreme Court proclaimed himself a
Zionist and said he would like to see Palestine under the joint
governance of the United States and Britain.[1]

The idea of a Jewish national home met with a mixed
reception in the United States during the era of the First World
War. Brandeis was intent on gaining American acceptance of the
declaration in 1917 and arranged meetings between Zionist leaders
and President Woodrow Wilson. He became convinced that the
president supported a Jewish national home in Palestine. But
some leaders of the American Jewish community were unhappy about
Brandeis' activities and at the end of September 1917 the
prominent philanthropist Jacob H. Schiff avowed that he was
concerned that Zionists talked about a Jewish national home but
really intended an independent Jewish state. Admitting that men
like Brandeis held a lofty conception of American citizenship he
nevertheless considered Zionism a danger in that it could lead

to a situation where American Jews might be torn between loyalty to the United States and a Jewish state; he accepted the idea of an autonomous Palestine under British rule, and had no objection to such an entity becoming a Jewish country if it remained a part of the British empire in the same way the Transvaal was at that time part of the empire. He wanted the Zionist leadership to declare publicly that it accepted such a plan and had no intention of using a national home as a first move toward an independent Jewish state.[2]

Official American concern over Palestine was slow in making an appearance in 1917-1918, for President Wilson moved cautiously --there was divided Jewish opinion, and the State Department opposed the Balfour Declaration in the belief that it would antagonize the Arabs. Wilson in August 1918 finally wrote the Zionist leader Rabbi Stephen S. Wise expressing satisfaction with the progress of the Zionist movement, but it was not until March 2, 1919 that he announced support for the declaration, that the government and people of the United States agreed with the Allies that a Jewish commonwealth should be established in Palestine. Later fearing that the phrase "Jewish commonwealth" went a step farther than the term in the declaration, "Jewish national home" he amended his statement, remarking that he only intended to show interest in the declaration.[3]

Meanwhile, with the war over, it became apparent that the British government had made several contradictory commitments concerning the Middle East. Consider the British promise to the Arabs. When the Ottoman Khalif had proclaimed a Holy War against

the Allies at the end of 1914, the ruler of the Hejaz, Sharif
Hussain of Mecca, had refused to accept the proclamation and
revolted against the Turks, and prior to the revolt his eldest
son, the Emir Abdullah, entered negotiations with the British
and after an exchange between the Sharif and the British
commissioner in Egypt, Sir Henry McMahon, the Arabs believed they
had been promised independence at the end of the war. In his
memoirs Lloyd George paid tribute to Hussain's men, saying that
although the Arab force raised was small it served well.[4] The
wartime prime minister thereby reinforced the feeling of the
Arabs that a promise was a promise. In addition to the
understanding of 1916 with the Sharif the British had reached an
accord with the French that same year on postwar spheres of
influence in the Middle East, an accord known as the Sykes-Picot
Agreement; it provided that some portions of Palestine would be
part of both the British and French spheres in the Middle East.
At an Anglo-French conference in London in December 1916 the
French offered to attach a battalion of troops to the British
Middle East forces. Lloyd George postponed accepting this offer
until British troops fighting against the Turks entered
Palestine, so that during the subsequent fight for Palestine
only token French forces were engaged, but the British promise
to the French, if not backed by a military contribution in
Palestine (as in the case of the Arabs), was an agreement between
two great powers and despite its conflict with the Hussain-
McMahon agreement it was awkward to disavow.

It is an interesting fact that during the First World War

there was effort to bring about an agreement between the Zionists
and the Arabs, although the effort was largely unofficial. Prior
to the Paris Peace Conference the president of the World Zionist
Organization, Chaim Weizmann, who thirty years later became the
first president of the State of Israel, conferred with the second
son of the Sharif, the Emir Feisal, a meeting between two friends
of Britain; the urbane Russian-Jewish scientist had settled in
Manchester and won the respect of political leaders and Feisal
the desert warrior had earned the gratitude of the British
military. Involved at that time in an attempt to set up an Arab
government in Damascus, Feisal was willing to accept the Balfour
Declaration in return for a promise of Zionist economic
assistance, and in signing an agreement with Weizmann he added a
proviso that the understanding would be cancelled in event the
Arabs did not obtain independence in Syria. Alas, the agreement
between the Zionists and the Arabs soon failed, although not
because of a failure of Jewish-Arab relations. Weizmann later
told an audience at the Metropolitan Opera House in New York
that the Jewish people understood the aspirations of the Arab
nation and that the Jewish national home would be established
without encroaching on Arab interests; it was all very simple--
the center of Arab national life was not Jerusalem but Damascus,
Cairo, and Baghdad, and the center of Jewish life was Jerusalem.[5]
The problem at that time lay with the great powers, Britain and
France. France was willing to ignore the Sykes-Picot agreement
to the extent of allowing British control of Palestine, but
insisted that Britain honor the provision giving France authority

in Syria and Lebanon. Feisal in 1920 then was forced to flee
Syria. The British soon established him on the Iraqi throne,
but damage to Arab pride never resolved. The chance for Arab-
Jewish agreement was lost in a swirl of later developments, of
confusions and misapprehensions that turned into hatreds, not to
be allayed.

In the years after the World War of 1914-1918 the history
of the Middle East moved inexorably towards antagonism. At the
Peace Conference in 1919, President Wilson was concerned about
fair treatment of the Arabs but found helping them difficult.
He was skeptical of their representatives in Paris; the Arabs
were not well represented, and after speeches by members of a
pro-French Arab delegation he learned that the chairman of the
group lived in France and had not visited Syria in thirty years.[6]
In keeping with his interest in self-determination the president
suggested that Britain, France, and the United States send
representatives to the Middle East to ascertain wishes of the
inhabitants, and an American group known as the King-Crane
Commission went out. Bound by the Sykes-Picot agreement, Britain
and France did not join the United States in the investigation,
and not much could be accomplished. The Americans concluded that
only the then 65,000 Jewish inhabitants of Palestine favored a
Jewish national home, while the half million Arab residents,
Christian as well as Moslem, desired unity with Syria. The King-
Crane Commission reported its findings but by that time the
United States was in the process of removing itself from world
affairs and the commission's work was ignored.

7

After the end of the World War, American interest in the Middle East--except for missionary activity on the part of several American Protestant denominations--essentially lapsed. An Allied conference at San Remo early in 1920 gave a League of Nations mandate for Palestine to Britain, with a stipulation that the British government secure approval of the League of Nations. After the Treaty of Lausanne in September 1923 ended the war between Turkey and the Allied powers the mandate went into effect; the State Department became concerned over protection of economic interests in Palestine, admittedly slight. The ambassador in London delivered a note expressing interest in a provision in the mandate for equality of economic rights of all nations; the United States was interested in oil exploration. The British reply was that only signatories of the Covenant could discuss the mandate. The British government did not want the matter to end there because it was distressed by the postwar withdrawal of the United States from the affairs of Europe, and wished to encourage almost any involvement outside the Western hemisphere, so it accepted an American suggestion for an Anglo-American convention to establish the American government's interest in Palestine on a basis equal with League members, and the nonbinding preamble of the convention of 1924 included the Balfour Declaration and enumerated all the provisions of the mandate, in some minor sense making the United States an adherent of those instruments. The State Department, however, assured that the articles of this convention would omit any mention of a Jewish national home.[7]

In the years after the war the British found it difficult to make up their minds about what to do with the Palestine mandate, and here was a cause of trouble that increasingly afflicted Middle Eastern affairs. A British Jew Norman Bentwich, who served with the military administration of Palestine, wrote that it was abnormal to follow a policy of establishing a Jewish national home in a country inhabited by Arabs, a people with whom Britain desired ties of friendship. An indication of the strangeness of the situation was that until June 1920 the British did not publish the Balfour Declaration inside Palestine, and the people most concerned learned about the British government's intention last. The task of attempting to establish harmonious relations between Arabs and Jews was onerous. Lloyd George selected a prominent Liberal party member, Herbert Samuel, a Jew and a Zionist, to be the first high commissioner in Palestine, and Samuel understood the Arab view, for as a student at Oxford he had rejected the orthodox tradition of his parents--writing his mother explaining that if sons did not irritate their parents by exploring new ideas, "we should still be savages eating acorns."[8] The innovative Samuel won the respect of both communities in Palestine. Visiting Palestine in the spring of 1921, Colonial Secretary Winston Churchill reaffirmed support for the Jewish national home. At a ceremony on the Mount of Olives, the site selected for construction of the Hebrew University, Churchill planted a date palm, and the chief rabbi presented him with a small Torah, and Churchill said that a Jewish national home would benefit the world; he predicted contentment for the scattered Jewish race, success for the British government, happiness for all Palestinians, Moslems, Christians, and Jews.[9] At the same time he arranged for a partition of Palestine; Transjordan, the region east of the Jordan River, was excluded from the area of Jewish settlement, and the Emir Abdullah was installed there. The exclusion distressed the Zionists and did not pacify the Arabs.

One confusion led to another. The leading Palestinian opponent of the Jewish national home was Amin al-Husseini; educated at al-Azhar University in Cairo, he had been instrumental in inciting anti-Jewish riots in 1920. Samuel appointed him to the important office of Mufti, reasoning that responsibility would induce correct behavior, and Husseini said he considered Britain's intentions towards the Arabs honorable and promised cooperation but did not keep his word. During the summer of 1929 attacks on the Jewish population brought many casualties, including several American citizens. The immediate cause of violence in 1929 was access to two holy places, the Western Wall (then known as the Wailing Wall), and the al-Aqsa Mosque, but the underlying cause was Arab nationalism inflamed by the Mufti. Order was restored after British troops arrived from Egypt, but the situation thereafter was tense.

By the end of the 1920s when the Mufti was carefully moving against the Jews, the Zionist Organization of America, known as ZOA, began to agitate for involvement of the United States government in Palestine affairs, and a delegation conferred with officials including President Herbert Hoover and Senator William

E. Borah, chairman of the Foreign Relations Committee. Hoover
and Borah said that action would be taken to protect American
citizens in Palestine, and appreciated the gravity of the
situation, but would not agree to protect Jews who were not
Americans.[10] The chief of the State Department's division of
Near Eastern affairs said that because eight American citizens
were killed in Palestine the United States did not have to become
involved, and emphasized that the mandatory government, that is,
Britain, had responsibility.[11]

If the government of the United States still considered
Palestine a locality for Britain alone to rule, some officials
took the occasion of the rioting there to criticize British
policy. Borah some years earlier had been a member of the group
of "irreconcilables" who opposed the Treaty of Versailles, and in
the 1920s he wanted the United States to avoid political
entanglement and yet establish a moral example to the rest of the
world. At the invitation of the ZOA he spoke before a rally in
New York's Madison Square Garden in 1929 and said that in the
case of the Palestine riots the British had been stupid; assuring
his audience that the opinion of mankind would sustain the Jews
in their demand for protection, he avoided any suggestion that
the United States should render assistance.[12] This position--
castigating the British for not living up to their
responsibilities, at the same time refusing aid--became a theme
in the speeches of officials and a source of increasing
irritation to the British.

As the years passed during the 1930s the affairs of Arabs

and Jews in the Middle East showed no improvement, only
deterioration. The situation in Palestine turned even more
complicated after Hitler became chancellor of Germany in January
1933, for he began a program of the extinction of Germany's
Jewish population. He instituted anti-Semitism--economic
measures forcing the sale of property pauperized Germany's Jewish
community, signs reading "Jews not wanted" appeared in shop
windows, the Nazis removed the names of Jewish war dead from
memorials, some Jews were sent to concentration camps. In 1935
all Jews lost their citizenship, and many of them went to
Palestine. This large influx of new immigrants upset the Arabs
who now feared that they would be pushed off their land. Arab
leaders called for resistance, which led in 1936 to a revolt
against British rule. Violent acts against Jewish life and
property played a central role in this rebellion.

Concerned over the plight of their co-religionists,
increasing numbers of American Jews supported the Zionist
movement. Speaking at a luncheon sponsored by the United Jewish
Appeal in the spring of 1936, Secretary of the Interior Herald
Ickes saw no inconsistency between loyalty to the United States
and participation in the building of a Jewish national home. He
said that American Jews were giving their less fortunate brothers
a "new deal" in Palestine in the same way Americans for the past
three years had been trying to give themselves such a program.[13]
At this juncture Zionism became ever more attractive, as
persecution of the German Jews drove their more fortunate
brothers and sisters in the United States to do something to help

--this meant ignoring Arab opposition and intensifying support
for the Jewish national home. For both the ravages of the Great
Depression and restrictions of American immigration laws made it
difficult to bring Jews to the United States. American Zionists
petitioned their representatives in Congress to help the Jews,
and seventeen senators sent a telegram to Secretary of State
Cordell Hull in the summer of 1936 asking the government to make
representations to the British to fulfill their obligations,
under the Balfour Declaration, to the Jews. Senator Warren R.
Austin of Vermont, who ten years later represented the United
States in the United Nations at the time of creation of the State
of Israel, said in November 1936 that Palestine was conquered
territory disposed of by a peace treaty and the Arab claim to
ownership was invalid. His colleague Royal Copeland of New York
wanted the United States government to tell Britain of its
disapproval of Britain's failure to do its duty in Palestine.[14]

Despite such pressures in the mid-1930s the British
government showed every intention of continuing the mandate, and
a royal commission chaired by a former secretary of state for
India, Lord Peel, went to Palestine to investigate the causes of
Arab dissatisfaction and consider the question of the Jewish
national home. Speaking before the commission Weizmann pleaded
for continuation of the mandate; he described Palestine as vital
to the Jewish people and said that anti-Semitism once had stopped
at the Vistula but now had crossed the Rhine, threatening Western
Europe. Six million people--the Jews of Europe--were in a
precarious position.[15] In this appallingly dangerous situation

for the Jews the Arabs were unmoved. Even the Westernized Arabs
refused to see anything more than their people's nationalism,
their rights narrowly construed. Appearing before the final
public session of the commission a prominent Christian Arab,
George Antonius, expressed what was to become a refrain--the
Arabs did not hate the Jews, but after all they were the majority
and as such demanded an independent Arab Palestine.[16]

The Peel Commission put forward a plan for partition of
Palestine that would have divided the country into three areas--
a Jewish state, an Arab state, and an enclave including Jerusalem
to be retained by the British. The Jews were unhappy with the
solution, but influenced by Weizmann who considered it foolish to
refuse even if their area would be the size of a tablecloth, they
agreed to discuss the matter. But there was no room for
compromise in the latter 1930s. The Labour party leader Clement
R. Attlee, who was to become Britain's first postwar prime
minister, expressed shock at Weizmann's position; he considered
the plan proposed by the Peel Commission a concession to
violence, a victory for fascism.[17] Meanwhile, although unwilling
to take a public stand on the Peel Commission report, the
American government wanted to avoid Zionist hostility, and the
State Department protested publication of the report because it
had not been consulted and the report suggested basic changes in
the mandate. Then the Arabs, formally consulted, rejected
partition, and the British government abandoned the plan.

In a peculiar way at this crucial time for European politics
the principles of Europe became the principles of the Middle

East. Confident that his appeasement policy would maintain peace in Europe, the leader of the Conservative party, Prime Minister Neville Chamberlain, considered it logical to extend appeasement to Palestine. In truth Britain had lost its backbone; the government virtually stood aside while Hitler, committed to redress the results of Germany's defeat in the World War, withdrew Berlin's delegates from the League of Nations, openly violated the Versailles Treaty by enlarging the Germany army and marching into the Rhineland. The British government did not interfere with the conquest of Ethiopia by Italian troops directed by the leader of fascism, Benito Mussolini. In 1939, the year when both dictators completed the destruction of Spanish democracy, Britain at last began to change its policy of nonintervention, but it was too late. Meanwhile, as fascism tightened its grip on Europe and the position of Jewry thereby became increasingly precarious, the British government virtually closed Palestine to Jewish immigration.

The British were not all of one mind about what ought to be done in the late 1930s, and the Labour party opposed restrictions on immigration. Visiting the United States in April 1938, the Labour M.P. Colonel Josiah Wedgewood, a staunch critic of appeasement, said that abandoning Palestine would be too great a disgrace even for a Conservative government, and he wanted to see Palestine filled with Jews so that in the coming conflict with Germany, Britain would have friends. He told American Jews to press their government to remonstrate with the British government against closing the only possible haven for fascism's victims; he advised greater Jewish resistance, explaining that if the Jews opposed the Palestine government they would not be fighting the British people who wanted them to stand up for their rights.[18]

Neither such critics in the Labour opposition nor those within his own Conservative party, certainly not the Jews in the United States or elsewhere, could turn Chamberlain from his course in Palestine. After Munich the White House received 80,000 letters and telegrams calling on President Franklin D. Roosevelt to use his influence to keep Palestine open, and the legislatures of Pennsylvania and New Jersey adopted unanimous resolutions to that effect, and 194 congressmen, fifty-one senators, and thirty governors presented a petition asking representations to Britain to keep Palestine open. The British government ignored all expressions of dissatisfaction with its Palestine policy. Certainly, regardless of what was done in Palestine the Jews would remain loyal. But what would the Arabs do? Here to be sure was a critical question, and the British wanted to ensure that the Arabs, the majority of the inhabitants of the Middle East, would not join forces with the fascist powers.

Deteriorating conditions in Europe continued to affect Palestine. When Hitler ordered the orgy of terror against German Jews known as Kristallnacht--synagogues burned, heads smashed, at least 30,000 Jews arrested--no country moved to rescue the Jews. Determined to stay in Palestine the British government wanted to satisfy the Arabs and in yet another attempt to bring Arabs and Jews together in February 1939 the British sponsored a conference in London where the Arabs demanded abrogation of the mandate and establishment of an independent Palestine and the Jews insisted on the mandate and reminded the British of their moral and legal obligations. As expected by all sides the conference collapsed.

Then came the important White Paper of 1939. The British government looked at what it understood to be its own interests and in May 1939 issued a White Paper announcing that Palestine would become an independent state with an Arab majority, and that to this end Jewish immigration would be limited to 75,000 certificates (virtually visas, but called certificates because Palestine was under mandate) over a five year period after which everything would depend on acquiescence of the Arab population. The White Paper limited Jewish purchase of land. The State Department cabled its London ambassador instructing him to mention to the foreign secretary that public opinion in the United States and especially Zionist opinion was disappointed.[19] Essentially the State Department agreed with this move by the British government, reasoning that a Second World War was imminent and it was important to win the confidence of the Arabs --the dominant group in the Middle East, an area of strategic importance. Acting according to the rules of the mandate the British presented the White Paper to the Permanent Mandates Commission of the League of Nations, which ruled against it. London prepared to defend the White Paper before the League Council. War was declared suspending League activities, and Britain put the White Paper into effect.

The Foreign Office was concerned that the White Paper would

adversely affect American opinion, and the British ambassador in Washington avoided calling attention to so unpleasant a subject as Palestine. Churchill, now First Lord of the Admiralty, spoke against the White Paper but did not influence his colleagues in the War Cabinet who could point to the fact that the American government made no protest. Many Britons thought that a pro-Allied attitude on the part of American Jews might make it appear to the still powerful isolationists that the Jews were trying to bring the United States into the war in pursuit of their own interests.[20] American Zionists did indeed protest the White Paper, but their government was concerned with the coming war and the Jewish question was not a priority. Their friends occupied with other matters, the Jews had nowhere to turn. Powerless to bring about any real change in the situation American Jewry held meetings, raised money, and prayed. It seemed, at least at that time, that the White Paper would stand.

Throughout the Second World War the Palestine problem exacerbated the affairs of the British, and occasionally entered the calculations of the Americans, but reached no resolution, even in its smallest aspects. Friction over British policy arose after American entry into the war brought United States military forces into the Middle East. Soon at issue was not the question of the Jewish national home but oil--oil for the American navy in the postwar era. To a lesser extent Americans took an interest in the long-range possibilities of trade. Both countries, Britain and America, wanted to assure themselves that in the postwar period their strategic and economic interests would not be jeopardized. The British were concerned that the Americans would take advantage of their enormously powerful position of virtual world military supremacy to displace Britain. At the same time the Foreign Office hoped that economic possibilities in the region would convince the United States to cooperate with British plans for political stability. Loy W. Henderson, who served as American ambassador to Iraq during the war and then became chief of the State Department's Office of Near East and African Affairs, shared the British hope, and sent reports from Baghdad explaining that if the United States supported Zionists goals in Palestine, relations with Iraq would suffer and the entire Arab world would consider the United States an enemy.[21] There were similar commentaries from other American representatives in the region.

But as the war progressed rumors and then authenticated reports of massive atrocities by the Nazis against the Jews underlined the argument for a national home. It was no secret that as early as 1933 concentration camps existed in Germany and that Jews in these camps were singled out for especially cruel treatment. The first unconfirmed reports of mass killings came in at the end of 1941, and were verified by the Polish government-in-exile through the Polish underground. At that time neither the American nor British governments had any knowledge of a German order for extermination of the Jews, but in the summer of 1942 the representative of the World Jewish Congress assigned to Switzerland, Gerhart Riegner, received information from a German industrialist that spelled out Hitler's plan for the

"final solution"--the destruction of European Jewry. Riegner
passed this information to both the American and British
consulates, and it was transmitted to the State Department and
the Foreign Office. In November 1942, Undersecretary of State
Summer Wells told Rabbi Wise that rumors of Nazi intentions
unfortunately had been confirmed. More evidence of Nazi
brutality reached the Allies. Wise saw Roosevelt at the
beginning of December and gave him a document containing a
country-by-country analysis of the extermination; the president
was shocked to learn that two million Jews already had been
murdered.[22]

For this pressing reason--the Holocaust--the Zionist program
at last entered the calculations of American politics. To a
conference of six hundred delegates gathered at the Biltmore
Hotel in New York City in May 1942, the Palestinian pioneer David
Ben Gurion, who in 1948 became Israel's first prime minister,
proposed what became known as the Biltmore Program, nullification
of the White Paper and establishment of Palestine as a Jewish
commonwealth; the American Jewish community accepted the program,
and both political parties began to give it attention. As the
deadline for the end of immigration approached in April 1944,
Congress considered a resolution against the White Paper and
favoring establishment of Palestine as a Jewish state, but in
view of Arab opposition the War Department persuaded Congress to
shelve the resolution. In the presidential campaign of 1944 the
Republican party declared that the Balfour Declaration guaranteed
free Jewish immigration into Palestine, and denounced President

Roosevelt for failing to insist that Britain comply with the
obligations of the mandate. The Democratic party countered with
the same demand, as well as expressing hope for a Jewish
commonwealth in Palestine, and Roosevelt gave his blessing to the
Palestine plank in the Democratic platform.

Rescuing the beleaguered Jews in Europe was another matter.
From the beginning of the war until August 1941, Jews could
escape from occupied Europe, and in 1940 about 8,000 entered
Palestine. That same year more than 36,000 came to the United
States--about half of all immigrants for 1940 were Jews. Many
more needed sanctuary; the Palestine White Paper and American
immigration laws locked out most of the homeless Jews. London
and Washington looked into the problem, and all sorts of
solutions were put forward, including establishment of a second
Jewish national home in British Guiana or perhaps a large
settlement in Angola, or even Alaska. Then the Colonial Office
took the position that Britain had no responsibility for the
Jews; one official even expressed regret that the inconvenient
homeless Jews were not on the side of the enemy.[23]

Unfortunately the Jewish problem would not go away, and when
Foreign Secretary Anthony Eden met Roosevelt and Secretary Hull
at the White House in March 1943, Hull brought up the problem of
60,000 Bulgarian Jews threatened with extinction unless the
United States took action. Eden said that while Britain would
admit another 60,000 to Palestine, it was important to move
carefully before offering to take all Jews out of a country like
Bulgaria, because world Jewry would want similar efforts on

behalf of other Jewish communities, Hitler might agree, and few ships were available for such an operation.[24]

In April 1943 an Anglo-American conference to consider the refugee problem took place in Bermuda, discussions with the understanding that the United States would remain silent on the issue of immigration into Palestine, and Britain would refrain from requesting a change in American immigration laws. Nothing was accomplished.[25]

Apologists for the Allies have pointed to the fact that atrocities were attributed to the Germans during the First World War and most of them were never confirmed. They have excused British and American insensitivity to the plight of the Jews on the ground that defeat of the Axis had to be the sole concern during the war years. Now that both American and British archives for that painful period are open it is evident that more Jews were not saved simply because the Anglo-American Allies were indifferent to their fate. Delay seemed the best course. A British Cabinet Committee again looked at the Palestine problem in 1944, but by this time there was no longer danger of Axis success in the Middle East, and the committee decided, as had the Royal Commission of 1936, that given the intransigence of both Arabs and Jews a partition of Palestine was the most fitting solution. Nothing more happened. Preoccupied with winning the war, Prime Minister Churchill like Roosevelt had little time for either Palestine or the Jewish problem.

From the beginning of hostilities the Zionists pressed for a Jewish fighting unit within the British army and at the end of

1944 a Jewish brigade came into being. Such a force had
political implications; ever mindful of Arab opinion it was
opposed by the Colonial Office: but once Churchill succeeded
Chamberlain as prime minister the Jews renewed their request and
Churchill was sympathetic and eventually told Roosevelt that such
a force would give enormous satisfaction to the Jews and that of
all races they had the right to fight the Germans as a recognized
body under their own flag. He asked for the president's views
and Roosevelt had no objection.[26]

As victory approached in 1945, the Zionist leaders believed
that at last Roosevelt and Churchill supported a Jewish state.
The Arabs continued to insist on the White Paper, and were
supported by the Foreign Office--this was the case even though
most Arabs had not worked for an Allied victory, and the Mufti,
leader of the Palestinian Arabs, actively sided with the Axis.
The Mufti had damaged the Arab cause by writing Hitler in January
1941 that the Arabs could threaten Britain's transportation and
communication network in the Middle East. After an abortive pro-
Nazi coup in Baghdad the Mufti fled to Berlin where he was
assured by the foreign ministers of both Germany and Italy that
the Jewish national home would be eliminated. Using his position
as titular leader of 400 million Moslems he devoted his energies
to the fascist cause; he encouraged Bosnian Moslems to fight for
the Waffen SS, and even formulated a theory whereby National
Socialism and Islam appeared to share a common Weltanschauung.
Adapting passages from the Koran to conform to Hitler's
pronouncements he admonished his followers to join in the war

against the Jews.[27] The situation impressed Churchill, who declared that except for King Ibn Saud of Saudi Arabia and Emir Abdullah of Transjordan the Arabs had not made any contribution to the war, and in fact fought against the British in Iraq.

The assassination of the British minister in Cairo, Lord Walter Moyne on November 6, 1944 by members of the Lehi terrorist organization, a Jewish group, protesting what they considered Britain's betrayal of the Jews, sorely tested Churchill's sympathy for the Zionist cause. Unknown to the terrorists, Moyne, had recommended partition to the Cabinet before his death. Shaken by the murder of his friend, Churchill afterwards told the House of Commons that support for Zionism had to be reconsidered. The Cabinet Committee that had planned to recommend partition did not do so. The problem was left for the postwar period where it became the responsibility of the Attlee government, and in the United States, of the administration of President Harry S. Truman.

CHAPTER 2

THE DP PROBLEM

The aspect of the Palestine problem that caused the greatest
strain on Anglo-American relations in the years immediately after
the Second World War was the desire of a pitiful remnant of
European Jews to leave the Continent in search of a homeland
somewhere. Most of these displaced persons, known as DP's,
wanted to go to Palestine, but many perhaps would have been
willing to enter the United States, the nation with the world's
largest remaining Jewish population. Victory in Europe focused
attention on their plight. During the Holocaust it had been
possible for the world to ignore what was happening, but after
victory and the liberation of the concentration camps the
enormity of the crimes against the Jews had to be faced, the ugly
word "genocide" had to be thought about. Soldiers entering the
camps found piles of half-starved corpses, large inventories of
gold teeth, and a selection of lamp shades made from human skin.
Although the exact number was never established it has been
estimated that in May 1945 there were six million Jewish dead and
perhaps 100,000 Jewish survivors.

At first it appeared as if Prime Minister Winston Churchill
would help the Jewish DP's. The problem was raised in the House
of Commons, where one member said that because Germany was
defeated all German Jews should settle in that country.
Churchill said that the Jews had been treated with exceptional
brutality and it would be cruel to compel victims of such

brutality to return to the scene of the crimes committed against them. Although he made no reference to Palestine he pledged a special effort.[1]

It appeared as if the new American President, Harry S. Truman, also would help. At the end of April 1945, Rabbi Wise and a delegation visited Truman in the White House. On his desk the president had a copy of the message that Roosevelt had sent the annual conference of the ZOA, a meeting held at the end of October 1944; the message pledged the late president to support a free and democratic Jewish commonwealth in Palestine, and the Zionists considered this statement of support the most forthright ever made by a chief executive. Pointing to the statement Truman said the Zionists knew the policy of Roosevelt and he promised to carry it out.[2] Then Acting Secretary of State Joseph C. Grew told the president that although Roosevelt had been sympathetic to Zionism he had authorized the State Department to assure the Arab leaders that no decision altering the Palestine situation would be made without consultation with both Arabs and Jews; when returning from Yalta in February 1945, Roosevelt had met Ibn Saud at the Great Bitter Lake where he promised that the United States would not assist the Jews against the Arabs, and on April 5, only a week before his death, he signed a letter repeating the assurance. Secretary of State Edward R. Stettinius Jr. advised Truman to make a distinction between the problem of Palestine and the issue of Jewish DP's; warning that Zionist organizations would demand a Jewish state he cautioned the president against committing himself, saying that the subject should be handled

with care and with a view to the long-range interests of the
United States. President Truman did not immediately accept the
Zionist goal, but he was interested in the plight of those
refugees who had survived the Holocaust, and seeking a solution
to the problem he ignored Stettinius's advice. At the Potsdam
Conference in July-August 1945 he met Churchill and Stalin for
the first time, and although he had many concerns he took the
opportunity to discuss the refugee problem. He planned to ask
Churchill to allow more DP's into Palestine. Then came the
result of the British general election, the change from Churchill
to Clement R. Attlee, and the opportunity passed.

Because the victorious Labour party had opposed the White
Paper of 1939, the Zionists looked to the new prime minister, for
at its annual conference in December 1944 the National Executive
of the party accepted a declaration on Palestine: "There is
surely neither hope nor meaning in a Jewish national home, unless
we are prepared to let Jews, if they wish, enter this tiny land
in such numbers as to become a majority." The declaration
suggested that Arabs move out as Jews moved in, a suggestion far
beyond any proposal ever made by the Zionist organization.[3]
Party members reminded the House of Commons of Labour's stand on
the question and of Labour's warning to the government in 1939
that a Labour government would not be obligated to the White
Paper. One member spoke of Britain's responsibility for the
Jews, saying that if only they had been taken out of Europe
during the war they could have lived happily with their people in
Palestine, but the door was shut in their faces. Yet Attlee did

not reverse the Palestine policy of the previous government, and indeed he told the House at the end of August 1945 that he had been in power too short a time to be able to discuss Palestine.[4]

All the while the DP situation was worsening. In the summer of 1945, Earl G. Harrison, dean of the University of Pennsylvania law school and a former Commissioner of Immigration and Naturalization, was investigating the Jewish DP's and reported to the president that the first need of these people was recognition of their status as Jews. Pointing out that most of them had spent years in the worst of the concentration camps, where they witnessed the murder of loved ones and often were the sole survivors of their families, he said their condition was far worse than that of other groups among the DP's. Harrison called attention to the Labour party's pre-election stand on immigration into Palestine, and expressed the opinion that most Jewish DP's wanted to go to Palestine. While he recommended that Truman support a Jewish Agency petition that the British government immediately issue 100,000 certificates, he also recommended that refugees be admitted to the United States.

Truman was moved by the Harrison report, and sought to bring the problem to Prime Minister Attlee's attention, but the result was inaction. The president sent Attlee a copy of the report and pointed to the recommendation for 100,000 certificates; Attlee replied that although his government sympathized with Harrison's views, the suggestions needed more thought. Referring to both the White Paper and to the late President Roosevelt's promise to Ibn Saud to consult with the Arabs, he stressed that Britain alone was responsible for order in Palestine and warned that 100,000 more Jews would cause problems throughout the Middle East. Years later he wrote in his memoirs that if Britain had placed the Jews among the DP's in a special racial category at the head of the DP queue, anti-Semitism would have increased.[5]

Here essentially was a rejection, and Attlee was concerned about its effect on American opinion; he wanted the Harrison report kept confidential. He said that publication of the report would harm Anglo-American relations, and was pleased to learn from Foreign Secretary Ernest Bevin that Secretary of State James F. Byrnes, who replaced Stettinius in June, was recommending to the president that in deference to Britain no public statement be made.[6] Yet on September 30 the American press published accounts of Harrison's recommendations and Truman's letter to Attlee asking for 100,000 certificates. It appears that the president was not directly responsible for releasing the letter. At a meeting on September 16 with three Zionist supporters, former Senator Guy M. Gillette, Senator Ralph O. Brewster, and Senator Warren G. Magnuson, the president mentioned the letter but said he was speaking confidentially and nothing was to be said publicly. His wishes were ignored.[7]

From the time of the Harrison report in 1945 until British withdrawal from Palestine three years later, the Cabinet in London insisted that the United States should not require Britain to solve the refugee problem without American participation. The British had so few resources with which to help the refugees, and the Americans were capable of doing so much. Home Secretary

James C. Ede read a statement in the Commons in November 1945
expressing the government's willingness to admit DP's who had
relatives in Britain; despite the desperate housing shortage in
Britain the British people would do their best to provide for the
homeless, and he hoped other countries would take DP's to the
extent of their resources.[8] Conditions in Britain made it
impossible for the government to offer haven to more than a few
refugees. Food was so short that even traditionally stiff upper
lips drooped--as when forty night-nurses at St. Bartholomew's
hospital in London remained in their beds an extra hour to call
attention to their scanty rations.[9] It seemed only reasonable
that the richest nation in the world should take action to help
the refugees; as one British visitor noted, perhaps with
exaggeration, there was enough food wasted in New York City in
one night to feed England for one week.[10]

Could the Americans have taken the refugees? Immigration
laws drawn up in the 1920s prohibited any large-scale welcoming.
Embarrassment appeared in a message from Secretary Byrnes to the
American embassy in London; he defended American immigration
policy, saying that no other country's laws were as liberal, no
other country could show a volume of immigration comparable to
that of the United States, and suggested that if the occasion was
appropriate ambassador W. Averell Harriman should explain that
the United States was willing to accept immigrants to the extent
of its legal quota.[11] He remained silent on the crucial question
of relaxing the regulations that excluded most refugees. It was
a curious situation. Congress was considering measures to reduce

immigration; supporters of such legislation said the refugees might take jobs from returning war veterans, occupy the low rent housing, and perhaps be degenerates, criminals, or subversives; it hence would be impossible to turn them into good Americans.

The British government was not sympathetic with the American quandary, and there followed a complex negotiation between London and Washington at the outset of which Chancellor of the Exchequer Hugh Dalton told the Cabinet that the United States should be pressed to take its share.[12] Bevin reported that he had proposed to Byrnes that Arab opposition to admission of Jews to Palestine would lessen if there was an early announcement that the United States would admit a substantial number, and he asked Harriman in August 1946 to find out if Truman was prepared to recommend to Congress admission of more immigrants. In a statement to the press the White House announced the president's intention to seek legislation. Bevin reported to the Cabinet at the end of October that there was reason to believe the Americans would indeed admit DP's.[13] He was disappointed in November 1946 when he attended the Foreign Ministers Conference in New York and cabled Attlee that he pressed Byrnes but was unable to pin him down. He assured the prime minister he was determined to keep pressing because immigration was an issue with which the Americans could help.[14]

President Truman wanted his government to do something and in his January 1947 State of the Union Message urged Congress to move quickly. Many bills were presented calling for an easing of restrictions; one measure, put forward by New York Congressman

Emanuel Celler, called for a law to permit aliens already in the United States on visitors' permits, unable to return to their countries of origin because of the war, to remain as permanent residents. Such a law would have benefitted very few refugees, and would have done nothing for those remaining in the DP camps, but Celler's measure never came out of committee. Most of the measures presented shared the same fate. Life magazine said it was shocking that the United States had the means to open the door to refugees but refused to do so, and an editorial in the Saturday Evening Post underlined the selfishness of the American position, pointing out that a nation whose population is mainly immigrants and their descendants cannot maintain that the only "good" immigrants are those already here.[15]

There was hope that Congress would act, but nothing came of it. A measure to admit 400,000 DP's over a four-year period, introduced by Congressman William Stratton of Illinois, received support. Secretary of War Robert H. Patterson favored it, saying that the War Department cared for refugees in the American zones of occupation, that it was difficult to maintain law and order, and expensive to provide food and housing--the camps, he said, were a burden. Spokesmen for the American Federation of Labor, the Congress of Industrial Organizations, and the Department of Labor related that new workers would not change the labor force to any extent harmful to the present workers. A spokesman for the Federal Housing Administration said 400,000 newcomers would not affect housing. Opposition from the American Legion and the Veterans of Foreign Wars was heavy; these organizations contended that the United States already did its share, and suggested that the DP's be let loose in Austria and Germany to fend for themselves.[16] The Stratton measure died in committee. Despite Truman's commitment to bring DP's to the United States he was unable to move Congress. The Displaced Persons Act did not pass until June 1948, too late to have any effect on the Palestine problem.

Delay over the Jewish DP's was an irritant to Anglo-American relations. In Parliament in February 1947, Bevin pleaded for help, calling the situation a tragedy.[17] On this issue the foreign secretary had the last word.

It is interesting that the impasse on the refugees threatened congressional passage of the $3,750 million loan to Britain requested by the president at the end of January 1946. Even without Palestine there was opposition; a public opinion poll showed a majority of Americans opposed it. They were represented in Congress by prewar isolationists and by spokesmen for business who wanted nothing to do with loans to a socialist government, and in addition there was distrust of Britain's system of imperial preference. But when to this opposition one added the DP issue it was too much. At Bournemouth the outspoken Bevin addressed the forty-fifth annual Labour party conference in June 1946. Most of the Labour party leaders appeared in a mood for celebration--Attlee wore a red straw hat, members of the Cabinet danced a Scottish reel. Then, alas, Bevin said there had been agitation in the United States, particularly in New York, for admission of 100,000 Jews into Palestine, and he hoped he would not be misunderstood if he said the reason was that Americans did not want too many Jews in New York. The remark deeply offended Zionists and many Americans who were not Zionists. The Foreign Office informed the British ambassador in Washington, Lord Inverchapel, that it was impromptu, and Bevin said he had been trying to put forward a constructive approach; he thought that if his speech was read in entirety the criticism would subside.[18] Such was not the case, for almost the full text was published in the New York Times, without any effect on the criticism against Bevin and the British government.

Something had to be done about the Bournemouth speech so as to save the British loan. Initially Bevin appeared unconcerned on the ground that he opposed getting upset with Jewish agitation, but when he received a cable from New York Senators Robert F. Wagner and James M. Mead expressing shock and comparing the speech to Nazi propaganda he agreed that the Foreign Office was justified in considering a reply.[19] The State Department wanted the British government to issue a statement of sympathy for the Jews. In his memoirs Attlee explained that Britain had to have the loan because without it he would have had to ask for hardships on a scale no leader had a right to ask of the British people at the end of a long war.[20] More than a year after victory, living conditions in Britain remained extremely difficult. A week's rations allowed one egg, an ounce of bacon, and six ounces of butter; the standard loaf of bread had shrunk from two pounds to three-quarters of a pound. Clothing was short, and when the press reported the satisfaction of a retiring quartermaster general with the clothing issued to him on demobilization--a suit, raincoat, one pair of socks, two collars, a tie, a pair of shoes, two shirts--there was an outcry because such a wardrobe would have taken more than a year's ration coupons. The War Office sent an officer to take back one shirt. A visitor to Britain in June 1946 reported that the public buildings were shabby and the cities grim. It was understandable that Labour leader Sir William Beveridge liked to spell squalor with a capital S.[21]

Despite the importance of the loan the Cabinet decided on no statement in favor of the DP's, because it would appear to have been intended to assist passage of the loan and probably do more harm than good.[22] The Washington correspondent of the London Times took the position that if some congressmen might vote against the loan to please the Jews an equal number might favor it to displease them.[23]

The loan passed on July 14, 1946. Support had come from an unexpected source, the moderate Zionist leader Rabbi Wise, a loyal member of the Democratic party, counseled American Jews to favor it despite British policy on Palestine. At the crucial moment Zionists supported it. But the debate served notice to the British that Palestine policy could affect Anglo-American relations.

The failure of diplomacy--and perhaps it was the failure of the American Congress to solve the problem of Jewish DP's--now began to lead into trouble, into the problem of illegal immigration to Palestine. Here was the most difficult aspect of

the DP problem, for thousands of Jews were trying to enter
Palestine illegally.

The problem of illegal immigration was essentially
uncomplicated. Many American Jews wanted to bring their
relatives into the United States, but otherwise favored a closed
door policy; this did not mean that they were indifferent to
suffering; they wanted to help so they financed the flow of
illegal refugees into Palestine. Although the number of Jewish
immigrants set by the White Paper of 1939 had been reached in
1944, the British for a while ignored Arab objections and
continued to allow a monthly quota of 1,500 Jews. This token
number was far too small. Considering, however, that it was
doing its best, the British government was incensed by assistance
given illegal immigration by American citizens, and Bevin asked
Inverchapel to impress the seriousness of the situation upon
Byrnes, remarking the responsibility to prevent citizens from
engaging in such activities belonged to the United States.[24]

Americans in official positions did their best to stop
illegal immigration, and an initial attempt was made by the
commanding general of American forces in Germany, General Joseph
T. McNarney, but nothing came of it. McNarney on August 6, 1945
issued a statement that the United States had never adopted a
policy of using the zones of occupation as stations enroute to
Palestine, and all organized groups of refugees entering the
American zones of Germany or Austria would be turned back.
McNarney was ignored; urged by anti-Semitic incidents in Poland
and elsewhere (when a Jewish soccer team played in Vienna the

crowd suddenly shouted: "Into the gas chambers!") groups of refugees continued to enter the American zones of occupation in Germany and Austria.

It proved difficult for the American government to deal with the illegals. Soon after General George C. Marshall replaced Byrnes as Secretary of State in January 1947 he confronted a demand that illegal immigration stop, and agreed to look into the matter. After defeat of the Axis, Truman had described Marshall as the greatest military leader in all history, and insisted in December 1945 that Marshall come out of retirement to serve as special envoy to China, after which he became secretary of state. Still, the refugee problem was a matter that the able secretary could not immediately come to terms with; at a meeting of the Council of Foreign Ministers in Moscow in March 1947, Bevin during a private conversation protested the American assistance to illegal immigration, and Marshall was unwilling to discuss the subject, remarking that he was so new at political work he had not yet had opportunity to review the situation.[25]

The State Department later sought to satisfy the British that it was acting in good faith; on many occasions the British had complained about advertisements in the American press soliciting funds for illegal immigration and advising that such contributions were tax-deductible, and the State Department asked the Justice Department to consider whether the advertisements were in violation of the law and asked the Treasury Department to examine the legality of the promised tax deduction. Bevin became impatient and suggested that the United States find some method of showing sympathy with the British, such as canceling the

treasury regulation that made it possible for Americans to take

tax deductions, and complained to the American ambassador that

Palestine was poisoning relations between the two countries.[26]

Marshall wrote Attorney General Tom C. Clark asking for action,

calling attention to the reported approach to Palestine of the

illegal ship Exodus 1947, formerly the American SS President

Warfield, and remarking that the Justice Department should

determine if Americans were involved in outfitting and manning

such ships used to carry illegal immigrants.[27]

Nothing the State Department did seemed to stem the flow of

immigrants. Consider the case of Exodus 1947, which took on

dimensions unforeseen when the British government decided that

rather than send intercepted illegal immigrants to internment

camps on Cyprus it would return them to Germany. The embassy in

Washington told the Foreign Office that returning DP's to Germany

would cause massive protests in the United States, spreading far

beyond the usual circle of Zionist agitators.[28] Truman asked the

State Department to so inform the British government. Acting

Secretary of State Robert A. Lovett told the president that Bevin

was sensitive about immigration, and that a formal note would

probably freeze the British in their position. With Truman's

approval Lovett asked the London embassy to have the British

change their plans; admitting that the United States had

responsibility for the ship's passengers because illegal

immigration was largely planned and financed in the United

States, Lovett stressed that the British intention to return DP's

to Germany had resulted in a barrage of protests both to the
White House and the State Department, that the matter was doing
harm to Britain's relations with the United States, and suggested
that the British should use other territory--perhaps Gibraltar
or Malta--to accommodate the DP's temporarily. Bevin was
informed that Jewish organizations in the United States would pay
the cost, and Lovett predicted that although Britain would be
criticized for such a solution the criticism would be minor
compared to the uproar from returning the Jews to Germany.[29]
Ambassador Inverchapel agreed with the Americans that carrying
out his government's plan to send Exodus 1947 to Germany would be
a mistake. From his arrival in Washington in May 1946 he sought
to learn about the American people and understand their point of
view; he had accepted an invitation to spend a few days on a farm
in Eagle Grove, Iowa, where he weeded the strawberries and helped
with the dishes. He made clear to Lovett that responsibility for
Exodus 1947 belonged to promoters of illegal immigration. Lovett
agreed, but said American opinion was incapable of appreciating
such a point. Inverchapel told the Foreign Office that Lovett's
pleas to find another destination for the ship was inspired by
friendship, a desire to prevent a break between the United States
and Britain. On receiving Inverchapel's report a Foreign Office
official suggested that the government proceed as planned: "We
have already incurred all the odium we are likely to."[30]

The case of Exodus 1947 went on and on. The British made
some effort to avoid returning the ship's passengers to Germany.
The refugees had embarked from France with forged Colombian visas

and without French clearance, and after Britain announced its intention to return the DP's to Germany the French offered asylum; rejecting the offer the DP's insisted they wanted to go to Palestine. The British government asked American assistance to convince the French to agree to forceful disembarkation on French soil; refusing, the United States informed the French that it would appreciate anything that could be done to ease the situation. Since the British had assisted the Arabs in pushing the French out of Lebanon after the war, France wanted to embarrass Britain.

Eventually the DP's had to return to Germany, and Americans were outraged. Former New York governor Herbert H. Lehman called the return a cruel, inhuman act, and leaders of the Union of Orthodox Jewish Congregations sent a message to their 3,000 synagogues in the United States asking congregants to pray for the British who drove back tortured souls who sought freedom.[31]

Many Americans were involved in illegal immigration; the Jewish defense force, Haganah, had established an American branch, not only to raise money but to purchase ships and recruit sailors, and one of the three men killed during the interception of the Exodus 1947 was a former merchant marine captain from San Francisco. An American correspondent who witnessed the arrival of the ship at Haifa, Ruth Gruber, wrote about young American sailors from intercepted ships who visited her in Palestine to talk of their experiences; they had determined to continue helping DP's, they said, and planned to return to Europe to run the blockade again.[32]

Commenting on the _Exodus 1947_ episode the British writer
Christopher Sykes later remarked that Bevin had fallen into a
trap set by the Zionists; another writer blamed the Foreign
Office saying officials were unable to cope with problems
affecting people beneath their own social class.[33] While there
was no excuse for the British government's behavior, part of the
explanation must be attributed to frustration with the American
position on refugees. A member of Parliament had stated the
British case a year before the _Exodus 1947_ sailed: "We must not
let them lecture us, and leave us face the situation we face in
Palestine."[34]

Soon after return of the refugees to Germany, Attorney
General Clark answered Secretary Marshall's letter regarding
illegal immigration. He said that many groups involved in anti-
British activities should have registered under the Foreign Agent
Registration Act of 1938, but advised against prosecution because
it would probably result in claims of discrimination and only
benefit the supporters of illegal immigration. Clark enclosed a
memorandum of the finding of the Justice Department that fitting
and manning of ships was a violation of law only if the ships
were to wage war against the British, and that "to characterize
the ships carrying these hundreds of displaced refugees as
vessels of war is to torture the fact." As to raising money for
anti-British activities, the Justice Department decided it was an
illegal act if such funds were used to purchase arms.[35]

The State Department did not want to have to deal with
another _Exodus 1947_, and leaned toward the British position. The

ship Colonial Frederick C. Johnson offered the Department an
opportunity to prove its intentions. According to British
sources the ship was in Norfolk being fitted for traffic in
illegal immigration. The United States Customs Service cited the
case of Exodus 1947, stating that before the latter ship left
American waters it was known that it probably would carry
illegal immigrants, but because it complied with United States
statutes it had been permitted to sail. The Coast Guard agreed
with the Customs Service that there was no legal method of
preventing clearance of the Johnson. The State Department
nevertheless ordered the ship under twenty-four-hour surveillance
and a Coast Guard cutter was ordered to use gunfire to prevent
departure.[36] Secretary Marshall informed Bevin that he told
Jewish leaders to stop illegal immigration or else he would
publicize the case of the Johnson. Several days later the State
Department told the Justice Department that Marshall would be
embarrassed if the press learned that the government was
preventing departure of the ship.[37] At the same time the owner
of the ship, Samuel Derecktor, who had served as a naval officer
during the First World War and had been a classmate of Lovett at
Yale, was pressing for release of his property. Washington
informed London it was reluctant to continue holding the ship.[38]

In the matter of the Johnson the British prevailed;
admitting that evidence against the ship was inconclusive the
Foreign Office underlined the critical nature of the Palestine
situation and said that because Derecktor at one time owned
Exodus 1947, the ship's release would entail an unacceptable

risk. Inadvertently Derecktor assisted the State Department by keeping the situation from the public; on advice of the Department he tried to convince the British embassy that the ship was not intended for illegal immigration. Here was an odd circumstance--an American citizen petitioning a foreign power to give him control of his property.[39]

The case of the Colonial Frederick C. Johnson became downright strange after the United Nations at the end of November 1947 voted to partition Palestine, and asked Britain to make facilities for immigration available by New Years's Day. The British refused, and the Foreign Office maintained Bevin's position that so long as London exercised authority in Palestine, it was axiomatic, that British immigration laws would be enforced.[40] The State Department asked Derecktor to post a $250,000 bond to secure release of his ship. He was willing to post $100,000, but called $250,000 excessive. Although his apparent willingness to cooperate made its position difficult, the Department decided that since the ship could carry about 5,000 immigrants the required bond would only raise the cost per DP fifty dollars, and the Jews had a great deal of money.[41] It was not until July 14, 1948, two months after establishment of the State of Israel, that the Johnson received permission to sail. Of course it departed for Europe and picked up immigrants for Israel--legal immigrants. Derecktor later obtained a picture of the ship in Haifa harbor in November 1948, and written on the picture was the message, "Mission accomplished."[42]

And so a great human problem worked itself out, largely

apart from the dealings of diplomacy, that is, on an unofficial and actually an illegal basis. The Jewish DP's found their own way to the promised land. The governments in London and Washington with the very best purposes, and the American people acting out of selfishness, had made it impossible for the DP's to leave Europe, the locale of all their troubles, any other way. It was a saddening situation, in which after the extraordinary exertions of the Second World War the two English-speaking democracies found it impossible to handle a human problem in a human way.

CHAPTER 3

THE FAILURE OF ANGLO-AMERICAN COOPERATION

If the DP problem was not solved by the Americans or by the
British it brought the two governments together for a short time
in an Anglo-American Committee of Inquiry. At first it looked as
if Washington would reject London's suggestion for a committee,
which was presented in October 1945. President Truman's Special
Counsel, Judge Samuel I. Rosenman, advised rejection, calling the
British proposal a "complete run out on the mandate." And then
Rosenman brought up the factor destined to complicate an already
complex problem--domestic political considerations. Referring to
the forthcoming November elections in New York he told the
president that such a committee would be disastrous.[1] These
views were taken into account, and Secretary of State Byrnes had
complained to Lord Halifax, the ambassador who preceded
Inverchapel, that Palestine was not even mentioned in the terms
of reference of the proposed committee. When Halifax explained
that London did not consider Palestine the only solution for the
DP's, Byrnes replied: "Jews over here are not interested,
apparently, in the plight of the Jews in Europe. What they are
interested in is they believe they ought to have a country to
call their own." Halifax said Bevin probably could be convinced
to make reference to Palestine in the terms of the proposed
committee, providing he was not put in the position of accepting
Hitler's thesis that Europe should be free of Jews. Byrnes urged
Halifax to do his best, pointing out that once on the committee

the Americans would be involved in the search for a solution instead of "sitting in the grandstand and shouting at you."[2]

The British government was reluctant to make Palestine the focus of inquiry of the proposed Anglo-American committee, but eventually gave in. Byrnes wrote Bevin at the end of October that Washington was concerned that an inquiry into conditions in countries outside of Palestine would result in too great a delay in solving the refugee problem, and as it was obvious that the two governments were unable to agree on terms of reference for the proposed committee, the idea should be shelved, although discussion could be renewed. Byrnes told the president that, as he intended, Bevin was disturbed by American rejection.[3] Then Attlee visited Washington in November to attend an Anglo-American-Canadian meeting on control of atomic energy. He crossed the Atlantic in twenty hours in a Douglas Skymaster, and on the first postwar Armistice Day the president escorted the prime minister to ceremonies at Arlington National Cemetery where they laid chrysanthemum wreaths on the tomb of the unknown soldier. Later at a private meeting Attlee agreed that Palestine should become the focus of the proposed committee, for he considered such acceptance the only means of obtaining American participation.[4]

From the beginning it was clear that cooperation was at best tentative. It was apparent that London opposed opening Palestine to massive immigration, and equally apparent that Washington, or at least Truman, remained committed to Palestine as a refuge for a large portion of the Jewish DP's. Bevin announced the Anglo-

American Committee of Inquiry on November 13 in the House of
Commons. Repeating his position that the Jews should remain in
Europe and live in their native lands without fear of
discrimination, he reminded listeners that the mandate for
Palestine required Britain to encourage Jewish settlement only if
the rights of the Arabs were not prejudiced, and underlined that
Britain had never been able to reconcile the Arabs to the Jewish
presence in Palestine.[5] Truman on the same date announced the
committee in Washington, made no mention of rebuilding Jewish
communities in Europe, and emphasized that the committee would
examine conditions in Palestine as they related to Jewish
immigration.[6]

It is noteworthy that while the American and British publics
generally favored a committee, Zionists and Arabs--the peoples
most involved--reacted negatively. The British embassy in
Washington reported American opinion less unfavorable to the
committee than anticipated, and the American embassy in London
reported British opinion pleased.[7] The president of the World
Zionist Organization, Weizmann, wrote Truman that the committee
could not bring to light any new facts, that Palestine was
probably the most investigated country in the world. The
president of the ZOA, Rabbi Abba Hillel Silver, declared that
Zionists would not be bound by the committee's findings. Arabs
shared the Zionist view, but on different grounds; while the Jews
demanded the opening of Palestine to DP's, the Palestinian Arabs
together with their co-religionists in the Middle East demanded
that the White Paper remain in force.[8]

48

Despite Zionist and Arab misgivings, once the announcement
was made both governments turned to questions of procedure,
although even here there were difficulties. What would be the
proper membership for the committee, and how long it should take
to complete its work. The governments agreed to six Americans
and six Britons but the question of time proved troublesome.
Byrnes insisted on a limit, and Bevin appreciated the desire for
speed but considered it a mistake to make the committee work
under pressure. The American government prevailed and a time
limit of 120 days was set.[9]

Who would constitute the American half of the committee?
Byrnes told Ambassador Halifax that finding members was difficult
and that at all costs the United States wanted to avoid
appointing the wrong people.[10] It was agreed that no Jews or
Arabs would be appointed, and some effort was made to see that
those who served had open minds. Selection of the American
members was completed at the beginning of December, with Judge
Joseph C. Hutcheson of the Fifth Circuit Federal Court of Houston
appointed chairman. Other members were James G. McDonald, former
League of Nations High Commissioner for German Refugees, later
the first ambassador to Israel; Frank W. Buxton, editor of the
Boston Herald; Frank Aydelotte, director of the Institute of
Advanced Study at Princeton; and William Phillips, former
ambassador to Italy. The last American selected was Bartley C.
Crum, a Republican lawyer from San Francisco, who from the
beginning generated controversy. Later Loy Henderson said that
Crum was a security risk, but the only evidence was that Crum was

"a type of left leaning lawyer who was almost tireless in his search for publicity" and was appointed over objection of the State Department because of his ties with Truman's adviser on minority affairs.[11] Defending himself Crum wrote that the danger represented by a West Coast Republican who did not hold Communist party membership was possibly exaggerated.[12]

The British government had no problem selecting committee members; Sir John Singleton, judge of the High Court served as chairman, and other members were Wilfred Crick, economic adviser to the Midland Bank; Sir Frederick Legett, representative at the International Labor Office; Lord Robert Morrison, a Labour peer; Major Reginald Manning-Buller, Conservative M.P.; and Richard H. Crossman, a Labour M.P. who was to become the most controversial Briton on the committee when he became a supporter of the Jews-- perhaps because he had visited Dachau immediately after liberation.[13]

The members confronted the question of where to begin, and this point generated controversy, but as happened so many times the American view prevailed. On behalf of the Americans, Aydelotte visited Ambassador Halifax to say that because of the committee's concern for the Jewish people its investigation should begin in the United States, home of the world's largest Jewish community. Halifax described this move as prudent in terms of American public opinion, which was one of the factors to be considered and could get the committee off to a good start. The British co-chairman disagreed, and the Foreign Office told Halifax that the British public and the Arab peoples would probably lose confidence in the committee if it took evidence from American Jewish organizations before undertaking an examination of problems in Europe and the Middle East. The Americans continued to press for Washington as the starting point, arguing it would be wise to allow American Jewish groups the first rather than last word. The British capitulated. The Foreign Office prepared to meet any criticism of acquiescence to the American view by saying that because the committee was an Anglo-American effort its members wanted to visit both Washington and London before proceeding to Europe and the Middle East; from the standpoint of geography Washington was the logical starting point. The Foreign Office told Halifax the public was not to be informed that the climate of opinion in the United States had decided the scheduling of the hearings.[14]

Giving into the Americans annoyed the members of the British committee. Crossman, not yet a Zionist, said that "their motive we felt obviously was to lure us into a hostile atmosphere and submit us to the full blast of Zionist propaganda."[15] Judge Hutcheson understood these feelings; two days after a Senate resolution called for opening Palestine to immigration and establishment of a Jewish national home he told the British embassy in Washington that the resolution was no more than an expression of opinion to please voters, and said American committee members would not be influenced by Zionist agitation in Congress.[16] The president reassured the British of confidence in the committee by refusing to support the resolution on the ground that such an action would be improper before the committee made its inquiry.

American faith in the committee won over the British and
Halifax reported in mid-December that while propaganda continued
"one is left with the impression that the president and Byrnes
are becoming somewhat bored with the Palestine problem."[17] The
British government was confident the work of the committee would
proceed smoothly.

Hearings began in January 1946 and a few Christians appeared
on behalf of the Arabs, some Jews spoke against Zionism, but as
expected most spokesmen favored the Zionist position. McDonald
wrote that the most sensational testimony was given by Albert
Einstein "who threw bombs in three directions," critizing the
British, the extreme Zionists, and the committee.[18] In the
middle of January the committee sailed for London, and according
to McDonald, British members on board the Queen Elizabeth worked
for fundamental points: a new start had to be made in Palestine;
the Soviet Union was the overriding problem; the United States
would have to support Britain in the Middle East.[19]

The London hearings took place at the Royal Empire Society,
and Crossman noted that the most obvious difference between
Washington and London was absence of an influential British
Zionist lobby. While twenty-five Jews were Labour M.P.'s,
British Jewry--some 300,000--was not strong enough to form a
pressure group.[20] According to McDonald the numerous Arab
spokesmen gave the impression that they would not accept any
compromise.[21]

The committee toured Europe's refugee camps and was told

that the Jews were entitled to live like other people in a place
of their own--Palestine. Crossman said that even if there was no
Zionist propaganda in the camps--and such propaganda was
prevalent--the DP's would have insisted on Palestine.[22] McDonald
wrote in his journal that "if some way could be found to get
these fanatics into Palestine, it would be temporarily for the
good of the world, though what would happen afterwards I don't
know."[23] Some American members made press statements about the
refugees' desire to go to Palestine. The State Department
promised an inquiry but told Halifax that the American members
were only answerable to the president.[24]

Afterwards the committee traveled to the Middle East where
the uncompromising demands of Arabs and Jews were repeated again
and again. In Jerusalem hearings were held in the heavily
guarded YMCA building, in the same room where the Peel
Commission had heard testimony. Most disturbing was the
testimony of Jamal Husseini who called the Mufti a noble leader
and said that he would probably head the Palestine government
after independence. When Crossman asked about the Mufti's
collaboration with Hitler, Husseini replied that some people
called the last war a Jewish war and he had seen this written on
the walls of the London subways. In Lebanon the committee
members interviewed some Christian Arabs. The head of the
Maronite church expressed sympathy for Zionism, and spoke out
against creation of an Arab Palestine, saying that the Lebanese
people feared Moslem fanatics.[25]

Completing its investigation the committee went to Lausanne

to write a report. In a letter to his family McDonald said it
was a relief to walk in the street without a bodyguard, commented
on the beautiful spring, and expressed fear that the committee
would not agree.[26] The difficulties were hammered out, and
during the signing of the report on April 20, McDonald, who
wondered why the British were willing to go so far to meet
American demands kept his fingers crossed, fearing a last-minute
problem.[27]

The committee report published on April 20, 1946 was a
compromise, yet all committee members supported it, putting
forward ten recommendations, three of which proved controversial:
100,000 Jews should be admitted immediately, the Jewish Agency
should cooperate to suppress illegal military forces and
immigration, and Palestine should become neither a Jewish nor
Arab state.

As soon as the report was published Truman angered the
British by ignoring Bevin's express wish, as well as objections
of the State Department, by issuing a statement that he was happy
that the committee had endorsed his request for immediate
admission of 100,000 DP's. He did not commit himself to the
report on the ground that it contained questions requiring study.

The British government had to decide what to do. Prior to
publication of the report a Cabinet Committee, together with the
British chiefs of staff, advised that the report might have an
unfortunate effect in India and would have disastrous
consequences in the Middle East. The recommendation calling for
admission of 100,000 refugees was considered unfortunate because

it repeated the figure proposed by President Truman and could be interpreted as a surrender. Before permitting Jewish immigration the Cabinet Committee suggested a disbanding of Jewish illegal forces, and cooperation by the Jewish Agency. Taking up these suggestions--although it is odd that he told his colleagues not to be disturbed by an initially negative Arab reaction--Bevin spoke to Byrnes during a meeting of the Foreign Ministers in Paris and made acceptance of immigration dependent on dissolution of Jewish resistance groups. Explaining that the Arab states opposed the Jewish Agency, he complained about maintaining four divisions in Palestine and asked for American troops.[28] Bevin's insistence on disarmament before immigration and his request for American troops did not imply rejection of the report. He told the Cabinet it was essential to learn if the United States was willing to carry out the committee's recommendations: "The essence of our policy should be to retain the interest and the participation of the United States Government in this problem."[29] But Truman's immediate public endorsement for the report's recommendation for 100,000 DP's changed Britain's position. Bevin according to his biographer Francis Williams was in a "black rage" because of Truman's statement, and first told Byrnes that Jews in Palestine were murdering British soldiers and repeated his objection to admission of Jews unless the illegal troops were disbanded.[30] Then the prime minister told the Commons that American cooperation was needed and the report had to be considered as a whole.

Anxious to begin discussion Attlee asked Bevin to take up

the matter with Byrnes. The State Department urged the president to adopt the report, and Acting Secretary of State Dean Acheson got the impression that Truman had agreed but before making a decision wanted to talk it over with "some of his people."[31] Then the president decided that the thing to do was to ask for Arab and Jewish reaction, and sent a message to Attlee that the United States planned to consult the Arabs and the Jews. Considering this an indication that Washington accepted some responsibility for the problem, Attlee was pleased. Bevin told the Cabinet it appeared the Americans would continue to work with the British: "They now seem to be willing to remove this question from the realm of propaganda and to study its practical implications on a business-like footing."[32]

But Arab reaction caused difficulty. Arab workers in Palestine called for a twelve-hour hunger strike, and in Jerusalem a mob left the Mosque of Omar shouting death to the Americans and British. The British had ties in the Arab world, and when dealing with Palestine gave weight to the attitude of the Arab states. According to one Englishman the Arabs were the only "race" the British admired.[33] Many Britishers considered foreign ideas not introduced by Britain as detrimental to the Arab way of life. Sympathizing with the view that the Jews were intruders in the Middle East, a British official in Saudi Arabia predicted Arab rejection of the report with the comment that the Arabs do not want the benefit of Jewish civilization just as some English preferred their own ways to American "gadget" civilization.[34] Arab leaders often warned London that it would be dangerous to support the Jews. Reporting a conversation with

Ibn Saud in January 1946 a British official said the king's

position would be difficult if British action in Palestine forced

Arabs to resist.[35]

All of the Arab states opposed the report. Secretary

General of the Arab League, Azzam Pasha, said Britain, at that

time in the midst of delicate treaty negotiations with Egypt,

could not escape responsibility. And in a strictly confidential

letter to the Foreign Office, which British representatives in

Jidda underlined was not to be communicated to the United States,

Ibn Saud appealed for delay.[36] Prince Faisel of Saudi Arabia

spoke for the united opposition that "surely the mutual best

interest in the area of 14,000,000 Americans and 45,000,000 Arabs

will prevail against the special pleading of almost 5,000 Jewish

lobbyists."[37]

But the Truman administration's ambivalence toward the

Middle East, despite some concern about Soviet activity in Iran

at that time, created a situation whereby the Arabs were ignored;

the American government showed far more interest in Jewish

reaction to the report. Zionists objected to the recommendation

that Palestine become neither a Jewish nor Arab state, but

praised the recommendation for admission of 100,000 Jews into

Palestine. The five million Jews in the United States were well

organized and constituted an important voting bloc.

At the end of May a rumor spread in the Middle East that

American members of the Anglo-American Committee had pressed

their British counterparts for immediate admission of DP's.

Washington charged that British officials in Arab countries spread the rumor, and Bevin moved to answer. The Foreign Office asked its mission in Saudi Arabia, and an official said the complaint was another example of American inability to accept unpopularity in the Middle East and that the source of the complaint to the State Department was an unnamed American official in Jidda who often loudly proclaimed his distaste for Truman's pro-Zionist policy.[38]

The rumor episode did no damage, but there was another problem; at the beginning of May, Crum announced to the press that Bevin had promised the Anglo-American Committee that if their recommendations were unanimous he would see to it that they were put into effect. The Foreign Office told its Washington embassy that it had no record of any such a pledge and to point out "the absurdity of supposing any minister could commit the Government in advance to a document that had not even been written let alone seen." Bevin privately admitted that he made the statement attributed to him, but said that Crum read too much into his remarks.[39]

Both governments agreed to press on, to come to terms with the committee's report. At the end of May, Truman appointed a Cabinet Committee composed of the Secretaries of State, War, and the Treasury, and approved the idea of a Board of Alternates for the above-mentioned secretaries who would go to London for discussion with their British counterparts. The United States continued to insist that Britain carry out the recommendation for immediate admission of 100,000 Jews. The president wanted to send an advance group of experts to discuss only the matter of Jewish immigration. Attlee reiterated that Britain would not determine policy until both governments examined all recommendations, and reminded Truman that a decision on immigration could only come after consideration of the political reaction, and military consequences.[40]

Meeting in London from June 17 until June 27, the advance group formed a plan for the movement of refugees, but while the meetings were going on the Foreign Office told Inverchapel that at every step in Palestine the government had to keep in mind the effect of action on neighboring countries.[41] Nothing was solved.

Meanwhile the Mufti escaped house arrest in France, which discredited the Arab cause. When news of the escape reached Palestine the Arabs declared a holiday, hung flags from buildings, and chanted support. King Farouk granted asylum, although an American intelligence team announced discovery of material in an underground shaft in Bavaria proving the Mufti's treason. Farouk requested that the Mufti refrain from political activity, but the Egyptian press said the Mufti's mistakes were noble and he should be allowed to continue his anti-Zionist activities.[42]

But British attention focused on Jewish terrorism in Palestine. Speaking to the Commons in early November 1945, the Secretary of State for the Colonies, George Hall, said terrorists were doing a disservice to their cause by continuing their campaign at the very time Britain was seeking a solution to the Jewish problem.[43] At the beginning of 1946 the British

government announced six outbreaks in Palestine involving twelve
deaths and 135 injuries. The American Consul in Jerusalem passed
on comments of British officials that condemnation of terror by
Jewish leaders was insincere, and reported that 50,000 Jews,
among them the Chief Rabbi of Tel Aviv, had attended the funeral
of four terrorists killed during an attack on a British police
camp.[44] As early as New Year's Day 1946 the Cabinet considered
action against the Jewish Agency, but on the ground that any such
action against the Agency would produce strong reaction in the
United States dropped the idea only to take it up again when the
advance party of experts was holding meetings.[45] Bevin said it
was imperative for the government to take action against the
Agency, but wanted the United States to endorse the decision.
The Cabinet decided to move but for security reasons declined to
accept Bevin's suggestion; it was agreed that the American
government was to be advised just before action.[46] Meanwhile
Bevin denounced the Jews, telling Attlee that Britain had been
their best friend and that the Zionists did not appreciate this.
Attlee sent a message to the president on June 28 that the
following day--Saturday, the Jewish sabbath--British forces would
raid Jewish Agency headquarters in Tel Aviv to search for
documents and arrest all leaders implicated in the terror; he
expressed regret for such action when discussion concerning the
Anglo-American Committee report was taking place, but pointed out
that the report called upon the Agency to resume cooperation with
the mandatory power to allow for suppression of illegal forces.[47]

     The raid on Jewish Agency headquarters followed by arrest of

more than 1,500 people underlined British determination to
connect the Anglo-American Committee's recommendation that 100,00
Jews be admitted to Palestine with suppression of illegal Jewish
troops, and once the action was taken the British were anxious to
sit down with the Americans. In Washington the State Department
made arrangements to speed departure of Cabinet Committee
members, and Inverchapel told the Foreign Office they would be in
London to begin discussion by July 12. The chairman of the group
was Ambassador Henry F. Grady, formerly Assistant Secretary of
State and head of the American group observing elections in
Greece; other members were Goldthwaite H. Dorr of the War
Department and Herbert E. Gaston of the Treasury Department.

President Truman now decided to accept the Anglo-American
Committee's report in entirety, and Judge Hutcheson and McDonald
went to Washington to speak to the Cabinet Committee stressing
the need of 100,000 certificates for Palestine. Truman told
Grady the United States would support all ten recommendations,
including provision, opposed by the Zionists, that prohibited
either a Jewish or an Arab state.[48]

At this juncture the British government changed its policy
on the ground that even suppression of illegal Jewish forces
would not bring peace. The British Chiefs of Staff stressed that
any plan would have to allow a military presence in Palestine and
be acceptable to the Arab states. The Cabinet decided that
during the forthcoming meetings Britain would put forward a plan
under which Palestine would have two provinces and a central
government.

Here was a new situation. The British considered how to
deal with the Americans arriving to discuss the report, decided
to prepare the way for autonomy, and the strategy succeeded.
Grady cabled on July 19, that the American members were thinking
along the lines of autonomy; the plan they were looking at was
almost a verbatim copy of the one submitted anonymously to the
Anglo-American Committee by Sir Douglas Harris of the Colonial
Office. It appeared to offer the only means of admitting 100,000
DP's into Palestine in the immediate future. Byrnes asked Grady
what advantage autonomy had over a partition that would put the
two parties where they would have to work out their differences;
and he told Grady the British were attempting to tie admission of
Jews into Palestine to Arab-Jewish acceptance of provincial
autonomy. Unaware that the British Cabinet had rejected the
entire Anglo-American Committee report he asked if London refused
to accept the recommendation for immediate transfer of Jews to
Palestine. Grady said only that autonomy was the best solution;
then too given the violent state of affairs in Palestine the
British presence was necessary.[49]

Meanwhile London was concerned that terrorists might strike
at officials regardless of where assigned, so all diplomats were
alerted to beware of anything unusual, to look for suspicious
packages. The Political Minister in Washington, Sir John
Balfour, did not think his name would shield him--the famous Lord
Balfour was his father's first cousin--and when a package was
delivered to his house bearing an unfamiliar return address Lady
Balfour called for help. Experts opened the package; the

suspected bomb turned out to be a tin of molasses.[50]

It was at this time that terrorism in Palestine reached a new high; members of the Irgun organization, under leadership of Menachem Begin, on July 22 blew up the portion of the King David Hotel in Jerusalem housing British Army headquarters. Among the ninety-one dead and forty-five wounded were Jews and Arabs as well as British. Begin later said that after milk churns filled with explosives were placed in the hotel basement, detonator and timing devices connected, warning notices hung in three languages--Hebrew, English, Arabic--a young woman phoned the hotel and told authorities they had thirty minutes to evacuate. According to the Irgun the Chief Secretary of the Occupation Administration, John Shaw, disregarded the warning: "This tragedy came through the fault of British tyrants who played with human life." Shaw denied any warning, a denial confirmed by witnesses.[51]

After this deplorable excess, members of the British Cabinet acted with moderation; one said it was important to remember the history of the Jewish community in Palestine, the background, and suggested that suffering created a pathological state of mind.[52]

At the same time the British government had no intention of giving in, and Attlee looked to the United States to speak out. The Foreign Office told the Washington embassy it wanted a strong condemnation; the British public would not understand silence when such acts were committed while Britain was working with the United States to settle the problem. Inverchapel pressed Byrnes for an immediate statement. The secretary appeared upset but told the ambassador to prepare for a delay because he would have to consult the president. Unwilling to accept postponement the Foreign Office instructed Inverchapel again to see Byrnes and urge an immediate statement. It went so far as to suggest it would be helpful if Truman declared that Anglo-American efforts were being "thwarted by this stupid outrage." When Inverchapel saw Byrnes the Secretary told him the president was about to issue a statement that was not all the British hoped for but was as far as the president could go.[53] Truman said he was sure every responsible Jewish leader joined him in condemning the bombing, that efforts were being made to solve the Palestine problem, and terror did no good.

The bombing of the King David Hotel underlined the urgency for a solution to the Palestine enigma. Grady forwarded the text of the Cabinet Committee's agreement on July 24, which reiterated the position of the Anglo-American Committee that Palestine alone could not provide a home for all Jewish DP's. Warning that termination of the mandate and withdrawal of British troops would lead to internecine warfare, it put forward the idea of provincial autonomy, division of Palestine into four areas, Jewish, Arab, the Negev and Jerusalem, with British maintaining partial control over Jewish and Arab areas, in addition to control over the Negev and Jerusalem. The following day Byrnes cabled Grady that it still was not clear when movement of 100,000 refugees was to begin, and warned that postponement of the movement of refugees until agreement was reached between Arabs and Jews would put the United States in "an almost impossible position." Grady assured Byrnes that the British did not expect formal approval from either Arabs and Jews but wanted acquiescence to the plan before allowing 100,000 refugees into Palestine. Dissatisfied Byrnes arranged a teletype conference with Grady, Ambassador Harriman, and Lowell C. Pinkerton, the American Consul in Jerusalem who was in London, and Henderson of the State Department. Ignoring the fact that his committee had disregarded the report of the Anglo-American Committee, Grady spoke as if that report was still the issue; he said the president had not segregated admission of 100,000 DP's from the other nine recommendations of the report, and asked Byrnes and Henderson to persuade Truman to refrain from pressing the issue. Byrnes asked what could be done to secure British consent for immediate admission of 100,000 refugees, and told Grady that in view of Truman's repeated statements supporting immigration the United States could not support autonomy unless the doors of Palestine opened at once, and that Grady should so inform the British government.[54]

Again the fate of the Jewish refugees was the issue. Portions of the Cabinet Committee's plan leaked to the press. McDonald met with the president and denounced the committee for getting involved in ghettoizing the Jewish community. Judge Hutcheson wrote to his five former American colleagues on the Anglo-American Committee complaining that the Cabinet Committee members had assured him before leaving Washington that they would consider the Anglo-American Committee report their Bible.[55]

Political leaders spoke out, among them Senator Wagner, who called the Cabinet Committee proposals "a device to stifle the hopes of a long-suffering people, even though it pretends to be a reasonable compromise."[56]

Evidence of anti-British sentiment in the United States increased. A British official attending a rally in Madison Square Garden reported his disgust at seeing a Union Jack marked with a swastika. Inverchapel explained to the Foreign Office that so much emotion was generated by the issue it was impossible for Americans to consider the facts.[57] Then the commanding officer in Palestine, General Sir Evelyn Barker, wrote a confidential letter to his officers--a letter soon made public-- telling them to forbid fraternization between the army and the Jewish people, to punish the race by striking at their pocketbooks. Herbert Morrison, Lord President of the Council, told Parliament on July 31 that the government disassociated itself from Barker's orders, but asked understanding for the situation under which the army worked. That same day Acheson told Inverchapel that the Jewish population opposed autonomy and so did the political leaders of both parties. After meeting with members of Congress the president decided to reject the Cabinet Committee plan. Transmitting his conversation with Acheson to the Foreign Office, Inverchapel explained that "this deplorable display of weakness is, I fear, solely attributable to reasons of domestic politics."[58]

The United States rejected provincial autonomy because it did not solve the problem. According to officials in the Foreign

Office Ambassador Harriman was depressed by the turn of events when he saw Attlee in Paris, where he was attending the Paris Peace Conference, to inform him of Truman's decision. Attlee said British confidence in provincial autonomy was based on expectation of moral and financial help from the United States, and he was disappointed the American government was unable to support what in his opinion offered the only possibility of admission of 100,000 Jews into Palestine.[59]

So after months of effort and despite the unanimous report of the Anglo-American Committee, the Anglo-American attempt to find a solution for the Palestine problem together with the refugee problem reached a dead end. The British intended to stay in Palestine; their two considerations were maintaining Arab friendship and preventing violence--mostly Jewish violence. The British had initiated Anglo-American cooperation, and at the beginning gave in to the Americans, at least on matters of form, but then it was the British who were responsible for failure of the Anglo-American effort. The president had committed himself to resettlement of Jews in Palestine, a fact he made clear, and hence was in a position of needing results. Some responsibility must be attributed to Ambassador Grady, who understood and championed the British position but did not grasp and therefore could not defend the position of his president. Truman had accepted the Anglo-American Committee report. The British Cabinet was shortsighted in attempting to push a plan that did not meet the hopes of the United States. Failure produced a great deal of frustration on both sides of the Atlantic as well as in Palestine.

The British had to decide what to do. Several members of Parliament, among them the leader of the opposition, Churchill, wanted to hand over Palestine to the United Nations, but there was speculation in the Foreign Office that this was just the course President Truman hoped Britain would take because it would enable him to put off the question until after the November 1946 congressional elections. The Foreign Office suggested Bevin ask Truman to offer some new proposals. Bevin rejected the idea, still believing in provincial autonomy, and so the British government decided to go ahead. Attlee informed the State Department at the beginning of August that in absence of American support he would attempt to modify the Cabinet Committee plan, meaning no provision for 100,000 certificates. He said that violence in Palestine endangered the lives of everyone there, and that he hoped the United States hence would help with a solution.[60]

London planned a conference of Arabs and Jews, and invited representatives of the Arab states, the Palestinian Arabs, and the Jewish Agency; again there was trouble. The Arabs agreed to send delegates but stipulated that their representatives would not sit at the same table with the Jews; the Palestinian Arabs agreed to attend only if represented by the Mufti, persona non grata in Britain; the Jews agreed only if the British released the Jewish leaders imprisoned in the July raid on Agency headquarters, and if discussion would take place on establishment of a Jewish state in an adequate area of Palestine.

The Jewish decision in favor of partition complicated plans for the London Conference for partition was no new solution. It had been proposed in the Peel Commission report of 1937, and Bevin had considered the idea before the meetings of the Cabinet Committee of Experts. After looking at a scheme favored by the Foreign Office he pondered attaching part of Palestine to Transjordan, a loyal state, and allowing the Jewish part of Palestine to become independent. He decided not to pursue partition, believing autonomy should leave the way open for its adoption. When the Cabinet discussed partition in the middle of July someone said the details would be appropriate for the Cabinet Committee of Experts, but the Cabinet decided to continue supporting autonomy because the Anglo-American Committee had rejected partition. The Cabinet did not rule out partition, especially if it could gain American support. At the end of July the Cabinet members again discussed partition, agreed that autonomy was a step, and hoped that in the future Palestine would be partitioned.[61]

Everything seemed so full of confusion. In Paris during the first week of August the Executive Committee of the Jewish Agency, which had claimed all of Palestine, passed a resolution that the Zionists would accept partition and support a British military presence as long as it protected the Jews. The American government appeared to approve the resolution. But the British refused to endorse the idea.

Refusal of the British government to accept partition as the basis for discussions at the forthcoming conference does not

appear to have had any relation to the Arab attitude. Meeting at
Alexandria in the middle of August, the foreign ministers of
seven Arab nations--Egypt, Iraq, Lebanon, Saudi Arabia, Syria,
Transjordan, and Yemen--rejected partition, and asked that the
mandate be replaced by an independent Palestine with an Arab
majority. Bevin considered the Alexandria declaration a public
posture, no indication of the attitude of the Arab world and he
instructed the Foreign Office to ascertain the Arabs' private
views. Officials in Arab capitals were asked to advise the local
heads of state that His Majesty's Government wanted to explore
every possibility. Approached individually, the Arab states
expressed a range of opinion. The Iraqis opposed any plan that
could result in a Jewish state. The Saudis opposed partition,
although the British minister in Jidda suggested that the King
might change his mind.[62] Preferring to avoid the word partition,
leaders in Syria and Lebanon leaned in that direction.[63] The
Egyptian attitude was murky; the Foreign Office received
information from an unidentified police source in Cairo that the
prime minister personally considered partition the proper
solution but would not act on the matter unless approached by
the British. Another source said the prime minister opposed
partition, but that his government's principal concern was the
Anglo-Egyptian Treaty and he was anxious to avoid a clash over
Palestine. The British minister in Cairo said the Egyptians
would be flexible about Palestine if satisfied with the Treaty.[64]
Transjordan's position was clear; King Abdullah, monarch of
30,000 square miles of lava and desert, considered partition

followed by an exchange of populations to be the only practical solution but would not say so publicly because in case of partition the Arab area of Palestine might join Transjordan, leaving him open to the criticism that he supported partition for personal gain.[65]

At the end of August 1946 there was some reason for optimism that the Arabs might accept partition, given British encouragement. The Conference duly opened on September 10 at Lancaster House and it soon was clear that there was little chance of a settlement because only representatives of the British government and the Arab states attended. Representatives of the Jewish Agency remained in a nearby hotel. Addressing the first session, Prime Minister Attlee warned that the conferees would have to regard the Palestine problem against the background of world affairs. He talked about how much the British had done for the Arabs and asked for compromise. He said that London would present a plan for provincial autonomy, and afterwards the Arabs could put forward their plan. Arab representatives did not appear grateful for blessings bestowed by Britain, or willing to compromise. The Syrian delegate, Faris Bey el Khoury, said the Jews were not an Arab problem and Palestine was no place for its solution. Attlee turned the chairmanship to Foreign Secretary Bevin who tried to convince the Arabs of the merits of autonomy. The Arabs presented their own plan, which provided for a unitary state in which Arabs would control immigration but a Jewish minority would receive constitutional guarantees of their political and cultural rights. A committee of eight Arabs and one Briton was set up to study the plan. According to the Arabs the scheme was consistent with self-determination and they threatened to go home if it was rejected.

At the end of September, Colonial Secretary Hall called on an ailing Weizmann at his London house, giving the impression that the Jews might join the talks. It was not clear when the Jewish Agency would announce its intention. In Washington the Zionists urged President Truman to issue a statement in support of partition, but Acting Secretary of State William L. Clayton Jr. described the situation in London as delicate and said an American statement would be harmful.[66]

The conference adjourned on October 2 and it was announced that adjournment was to enable the British to study the Arab plan, but Attlee told Washington that the Jews were about to send representatives to the conference and hence the ending.[67] The Jewish Agency remained committed to partition. The Agency representative in Washington, Eliahu Epstein, said the Jews knew the American government could make Britain do its bidding, and asked for presidential pressure on the British government to admit 100,000 refugees into Palestine.[68]

Confusion momentarily lifted as American domestic politics brought statement-making by President Truman and his Republican opponent Governor Thomas E. Dewey of New York--not yet a presidential candidate against Truman, but looking in that direction. With the 1946 elections approaching, under pressure, cognizant that Dewey was going to speak in support of the Zionists, Truman decided to make a statement that would satisfy the Jewish Agency. Attlee was notified and Bevin wanted to persuade Truman to alter the proposed statement; he said he would explain that such a statement might provoke violence and could result in a British withdrawal. Attlee sent a message asking Truman to delay. He blamed the Jews for adjournment of the London Conference, saying that a decision could have been reached if the Agency had accepted an invitation to attend.[69] Ignoring the British objections, Truman made what became known as his Yom Kippur statement--on the eve of that holy day. He said the proposal for a Jewish state was favorably received in the United States, and immigration into Palestine should not be delayed.

Unsympathetic with Truman's political problems, Attlee was angry. He told the president that the Yom Kippur statement lessened the possibility that the Jews would join the conference, and that the British alone were responsible for Palestine. Truman apologized for any embarrassment, but said one of the purposes of the mandate was to assist in development of the Jewish national home, impossible unless Jews entered Palestine. He claimed that millions of Americans wanted something done about the DP's.[70]

The British government began to consider withdrawing from Palestine. Bevin told the Cabinet that if there was no prospect of a settlement by the beginning of December, Britain would surrender the mandate and pull out. He warned that such a course would endanger Britain's position in the Middle East, as well as affect Britain's prestige.[71] London and Washington began exchanging ideas about how to bring in the Jews and Acheson told

Inverchapel the president saw only a small gap between partition and autonomy. Inverchapel replied that even Bevin was moving toward partition, but would not support it without a commitment of American cooperation.[72] There is no evidence this was so. Meeting with Agency representatives in early October, Bevin did say he was trying to reconcile the irreconcilable, but suggested that since the Jews were the most adaptable people in the world they should find a way to live with the Arabs.[73]

Notwithstanding the Yom Kippur statement it turned out that the American government was not ready for partition. When Secretary Byrnes asked whether Britain would consider partition, Bevin replied that his government would not make a commitment, but suggested that Arabs and Jews receive consideration at the conference table. When the two men met with Inverchapel, Byrnes asked that no record be made and that his views be kept secret; he said he was anxious to assist in a solution and would try for presidential authority to press the Agency to participate in a new session of the London Conference, on British terms.[74] Afterwards Bevin visited the White House and told the president the Jews were difficult: "I tell them sometimes that I can no more fulfill all the prophecies of Ezekiel than I can those of that other great Jew, Karl Marx." According to Bevin's notes Truman apologized again and said that because the elections were over he would be more helpful.[75]

Delegates to the twenty-second Zionist Congress--2,000 members from sixty-three countries--met in Basle in the middle of December, the first such meeting since the Holocaust. The

meeting was simply not a proper occasion for any sort of
compromise. As one delegate wrote, "it was like the gathering of
a terribly bereaved family mourning the death of multitudes, but
rallying itself--despite its great grief--to save the remnants
and to face the problem of the present."[76] A group of DP's
arrived from Munich that included Reuben Rubinstein, formerly a
leader of the Lithuanian Jewish community. After years of forced
labor, and the death of his entire family, he was so changed that
friends did not recognize him.[77] There were many individuals
like Rubinstein at the Congress. As an expression of solidarity
with the martyred and the survivors, Yiddish replaced German as
the language of the meetings--even the diehard Hebraists agreed.
The mantle of leadership fell to the Americans who now represented
the largest Jewish community in the world, and the militant Rabbi
Silver, who scorned cooperation with the British, emerged as the
congress' spokesman. Weizmann pleaded for moderation, for an end
to violence, for continued efforts to work with the British.
London hoped for some indication that the Jews would be
reasonable, but the delegates voted not to send representatives
to the London Conference.

The British were in an awkward position and wanted to know
once more how far the United States was willing to go in order to
help with partition. It was clear that pleasing the Jews was
impossible without antagonizing the Arabs. At the heart of the
matter the question was whether Washington would make some sort
of military commitment.

It seemed unlikely that the United States would send troops

to Palestine, for Truman long had maintained that troops would not be used in the Middle East. Returning from the Potsdam Conference in the summer of 1945 he told reporters he did not want to send 500,000 soldiers to make peace in Palestine. He was under pressure to bring servicemen home; the issue was of such political importance that the War and Navy Departments were submitting daily reports to the president on the number of men released.[78] When Truman made his initial request in 1945 that Britain allow 100,000 DP's into Palestine he did not take into account the possible military problems. The State Department estimated it would take 400,000 men to keep order and the British would ask for between 200,000 and 300,000 Americans. After publication of the Anglo-American committee report Secretary Byrnes announced that the United States was not ready to make any military commitment. Later the American Joint Chiefs of Staff recommended no action that would result in a situation beyond the capabilities of British troops. The Chiefs warned that appearance of American troops would risk disturbances in the area, and called attention to the sizeable oil reserves, saying force would prejudice both American and British interests, resulting in an opening for the Soviet Union.[79]

Everything moved toward stalemate. Rabbi Silver said the Arab states had no right to discuss Palestine, and the lieutenant governor of Illinois compared the Zionists to patriots of the American Revolution. When the London Conference reconvened, Lancaster House was under heavy guard; two Britons had been kidnapped in Tel Aviv--one a presiding judge. More violence was expected. Officially the Jews were absent, but Zionists held private talks at the Colonial Office. For the first time representatives of the Palestinian Arabs attended--the Mufti remained in the Middle East but directed the delegation from there.

Bevin complained to the Arabs about the intransigence of the Jews, and blamed the United States for what he called misguided behavior. He told the Jews at the Colonial Office they were "cutting their own throats."[80] The atmosphere was chilly; relations were strained, and nothing was achieved.

Bevin looked for a scapegoat, and lashed out at President Truman for the Yom Kippur statement four months earlier. In the House of Commons at the end of February 1947 he said his attempt to solve the Palestine problem had been made the subject of local elections. Denying he wanted to cause bad feelings he said he felt so strongly he had to speak.

The timing of Bevin's outburst was odd; just four days before, the Washington embassy had delivered an urgent message to the State Department explaining that Britain's resources would make it impossible for the government to continue aid to Greece and Turkey after March 31, 1947, and that the United States should take over Britain's role in these two countries. Bevin was torn between the need to express his anger, and the necessity of good relations with Truman because of this new problem.

As a last resort Bevin decided to turn to the United Nations. The British government had grave doubts about giving the problem to the U.N. but there was nothing else to do. Bevin explained to the Cabinet that he had worked to find an answer, and had not been able. There was no way out but to appeal to the world organization.[81]

It was not clear what Britain expected from the U.N. The Cabinet told Bevin that submitting the problem did not obligate the government to enforce a solution. He hoped the Jews and Arabs would be more willing to compromise so that the question could be withdrawn from the General Assembly agenda.[82] The colonial secretary told the House the British government was not going to the U.N. to surrender but to set out the problem and ask advice.

CHAPTER 4

PALESTINE AND THE UNITED NATIONS

The United Nations Organization, domiciled temporarily at
Lake Success outside New York City, received the Palestine
problem early in the year 1947, when in the United States and
elsewhere there was still large public confidence that if all the
nations gathered together to act upon anything, certainly the
problem of Palestine, the sum of the nations would prove greater
than the parts. If initial confusion attended the councils of
the U.N., that did not seem to matter. The nations, acting in
their world organization, could focus on the confusion and bring
about a worthwhile result.

At the outset the U.N. gave evidence of doing something
about Palestine. Even before the special session of the General
Assembly at the end of April 1947 the Arabs had said that they
would press for a decision. Washington and London wanted a
committee to investigate the Palestine problem, and when the
session met the British and Americans prevailed. Then the Soviet
Union suggested that representatives of the Big-Five be on the
committee. Unwilling to give Moscow an opportunity to meddle in
Palestine, the Anglo-Americans were able to defeat the proposal.
An eleven-nation United Nations committee on Palestine, known as
UNSCOP, composed of representatives from Australia, Canada,
Czechoslovakia, Guatemala, India, Iran, the Netherlands, Peru,
Sweden, Uruguay, and Yugoslavia, was set up to look at the
problem, find a solution, and report in September to the General

Assembly. The Arab Higher Committee and the Jewish Agency were asked to send their representatives to accompany UNSCOP in an investigatory journey to Palestine.

It was uncertain whether Palestine might continue as an administrative entity, and the Soviet Union surprised observers in the middle of May when Ambassador Gromyko announced at the U.N. that his government's preference was for a united Palestine. If Jews and Arabs refused to cooperate, Moscow would consider partition. Gromyko spoke as if the Russian giant was the champion of the Jews; he accused the West of indifference, saying that not a single European state had guaranteed the elementary rights of the Jewish people or sought to compensate them for their suffering under Hitler.[1] Recent discussion with Moscow had convinced Washington and London that relations with the Soviet Union would be difficult, and both governments considered Gromyko's remarks an effort to take advantage. But the Jews were delighted with the Soviet position, and attempted to get support for partition from Washington, insisting that the Yom Kippur statement committed the United States.[2]

The Jews made plans to welcome the U.N. committee to Palestine and one terrorist group, the Stern gang, even printed leaflets saying the safety of the UNSCOP fact-finders would be guaranteed. The Jewish community wanted to do whatever was necessary to make a good impression.

The Arabs did not want UNSCOP or any sort of investigation and the Arab Higher Committee laid the groundwork for a boycott. Advising the Palestinian Arabs, the vice-president of the

committee, Jamal Husseini said that in event of a visit by
members of UNSCOP Arabs must show respect yet not take part.

Tension increased in Palestine as the country waited the
eleven-nation U.N.-appointed committee. Life was difficult for
British officials who were confined to compounds, known as
Bevingrads, surrounded by barbed wire, sandbags, and machine
guns. The few wives who remained ventured out only if
accompanied by escort, often Transjordanian legionaries. One
journalist complained that even if safety was not a factor there
was no place to go. Tel Aviv was unsatisfactory; it impressed
with its bustle but had no urban personality. As for the
countryside, it was arid and treeless. Some soldiers resorted to
strange charms. A young private carried a picture of the founder
of the Stern gang, Abraham Stern, in his cap. He explained that
it helped him feel safe. The British government put an airplane
at the disposal of officials to enable them to take short home-
leaves. Conditions in Britain did not lift the spirits and
Britons in Palestine opted for brief holidays in Syria or
Transjordan.[3]

The Palestine government made elaborate preparations for
welcoming the members of UNSCOP and fifty-five flag staffs, one
for every member nation of the U.N., were set up outside the King
David Hotel. Thirty-five chauffeurs were assigned to the
committee--one had served the Peel Commission in 1936, and the
Anglo-American Committee in 1946.[4]

All of the committee members were in Palestine by the middle
of June: John D. L. Hood, Senior Counselor of External Affairs

from Australia; Justice Ivan Rand of the Supreme Court of Canada;

Dr. Karel Lisicky, Minister Plenipotentiary of the Foreign

Service from Czechoslovakia; Dr. Jorge Garcia-Granados,

Ambassador to the United States from Guatemala; Sir Abdur Rahman,

High Court justice from India; Nasrollah Entezam, former Foreign

Minister from Iran; Dr. Nicolaas Blom, Acting Lieutenant

Governor-General of the Dutch East Indies; Dr. Arturo G. Salazar,

ambassador to the Vatican from Peru; Justice Emil Sandstrom,

Swedish representative on the International Court of Arbitration

at The Hague; Enrique Rodriquez Fabregat, former minister of

education, from Uruguay; Vladimir Simic, president of the

Yugoslav senate. The group was balanced, representing many

different points of view, and although Entezam and Rahman were

Moslems, Garcia-Granados and Fabregat were committed to the

Zionists.

Hearings began under difficult conditions. The Arab

population went on strike to demand an Arab state. A message

from the Mufti, which British censorship had kept out of print,

was read in all Mosques on June 16, in celebration of Mohamad's

flight from Mecca to Jerusalem. Calling for sacrifices the Mufti

demanded resistance. London ordered all public servants

scheduled to speak to UNSCOP to do so in private, and UNSCOP met

behind closed doors in the Jerusalem YMCA, in the room where the

previous year the Anglo-American Committee of Inquiry heard

testimony. Adding to the atmosphere of deja vu, the mandatory

presented the same material it had given the Anglo-American

Committee. UNSCOP's chairman Justice Sandstrom afterwards

broadcast an appeal to the population to present their views, promising that the committee would give the Assembly an impartial report. The Jews responded but the Arabs refused.

Dissatisfaction in Palestine was easy to discern. UNSCOP toured the country and saw evidence of the gulf between communities. Everywhere Jews greeted the committee warmly; when members arrived in Tel Aviv, banners proclaimed that the British should give up the mandate, and cheering crowds lined the streets. The mayor and city council welcomed UNSCOP on the steps of town hall. As the party was leaving the crowd started to sing the Zionist hymn Hatikvah, later the anthem of the Jewish state, while committee members stood at attention. The committee toured modern factories and schools and at one school Professor Fabregat sat next to a twelve-year-old reading an English text. Looking at the girl he remarked to a correspondent: "When I think the Germans killed children like these . . ." He did not finish the sentence.[5] Members of UNSCOP later went to the Jewish settlement of Revivim in the Negev; explaining how they had reclaimed the land, settlers pointed to fruit trees and vegetable gardens, predicting that if given the opportunity they could irrigate enough desert to settle millions of Jews.[6] But Arab areas were unfriendly to the committee visitors. When UNSCOP went to Arab factories and schools, mostly inferior to their Jewish counterparts, they were almost ignored. In one Arab school all of the children turned their heads as the committee entered. In Hebron the mayor refused a meeting but did escort the group to the Mosque erected over the burial site of the Hebrew patriarchs--holy to both Moslems and Jews. The mayor issued an order that nobody in the party of the Jewish faith enter the Mosque.[7] In the Negev, UNSCOP saw tattered tents or else virtually mud villages, and herds of goats. Arabs sat outside their frowzy dwellings and stared at the visitors. The children ran dissheveled through the putrid streets and pathways. Visitors from the world organization sometimes thought that their welcome, if such it was, had been organized in reverse--to show how the Arab community hated the intervention of outsiders in what they considered the dismemberment of their centuries-old right to live in the land that two millenia before momentarily had belonged to the Jews.

After seeing the country with what one reporter called the "grim pertinacity of an American tourist," UNSCOP heard testimony of Jewish leaders--an impassioned plea for a Jewish state. Weizmann blamed Britain for all the violence in Palestine and said the only solution was a Jewish state. Rahman asked if that solution would be accepted by the Arabs. Weizmann replied that the Arabs would eventually agree. Later Rahman pointed out that Jews had discriminated against Arabs by promoting a policy of no Arab labor on Jewish land. Weizmann told him that Arabs did not hire Jews. When it was Ben-Gurion's turn to testify, he said that partition was a sacrifice for the Jews who had wanted all of Palestine, but now were willing to consider a Jewish state in part of Palestine. Simic asked if he was pessimistic about Arab-Jewish cooperation. Ben-Gurion said no, but that as long as the Arabs thought that they could prevent Jewish immigration they

would refuse to cooperate. Judge Sandstrom asked what the
Haganah was and if it was armed. Explaining that the Haganah was
the Jewish community's defense force, he said he hoped it was
armed.[8]

Two members of UNSCOP had a firsthand look at the tragedy of
the Jewish DP's when the Exodus 1947, intercepted by the British
navy, entered Haifa harbor on July 25. Sandstrom and Simic
witnessed the disembarkation of the illegal refugees and their
transfer to deportation ships. Sandstrom reported that the DP's
looked poor and tired.[9]

At the end of July, UNSCOP went to Lebanon to hear Arab
testimony. Six Arab states sent spokesmen to testify before the
committee; all united in opposition to a Jewish state. It was a
picturesque meeting, with a variety of dress: the Saudis wore
white gold-braided headdresses, Yemenites carried curved daggers
in their belts, many representatives wore bright red tarbooshes.
But there was no variety of opinion. The Foreign Minister of
Lebanon, Hamid Frangie, spoke for the Arabs when he said that
every Jew who entered Palestine after the Balfour Declaration--
November 1917--would be considered illegal when the Arabs
controlled Palestine. Lisicky wanted to know what compromise the
Arabs were willing to accept. The Arabs refused to consider any
sort. They insisted on the end of Jewish immigration and
establishment of an Arab state. The committee went to
Transjordan where the same play was repeated.[10]

Everywhere during the committee's stay in the Middle East
the concern of both Jews and Arabs was terrorism, the extralegal

solution of their contentions. Neither side seemed to believe in the rule of law and preferred to take matters into its hands. Each side believed that in any local contest it could win.

The confusions of terrorism were inescapable. UNSCOP was asked by the families of three Jewish terrorists awaiting execution in Acre prison to intervene with the British authorities to save the young men. After considerable discussion the committee declined, but agreed to a resolution of concern if the sentences were carried out. British officials informed UNSCOP that the sentences had not been confirmed and it was necessary to avoid public comment until they were. Terrorists then struck at a Palestine government liaison officer working with the committee and attempted to kidnap him; he was knocked down and partly chloroformed before his wife's screams frightened off his abductors.[11]

After the committee members left the Middle East to visit DP's in Europe and then to go to tranquil Geneva to work on their report, new violence arose. When the military commander confirmed the death sentences of the three Jews the Irgun kidnapped two British sergeants, and as soon as the condemned were hanged the Irgun announced execution of their hostages. Following the murder some British soldiers lashed out at the Jewish population, resulting in the death of five Jews in Tel Aviv.

At the end of August, UNSCOP's report was ready. The United States and Britain both refused to approve UNSCOP's handiwork. The majority report signed by the delegates from Canada,

Czechoslovakia, Guatemala, Netherlands, Peru, Sweden and Uruguay
called for partition, with economic union, a two-year transition
in which Britain would continue administration of Palestine under
U.N. auspices, and immediate admission of 150,000 Jews.[12]
Beeley, whom the Jews considered "Bevin's pro-Arab Rasputin,"
called the plan unfair: Henderson, also disliked by the Jews,
told Secretary Marshall that many of his colleagues thought the
scheme unworkable, and warned of loss to the United States of the
great resources of the Middle East.[13] Meeting with the American
U.N. delegation Marshall presented the dilemma: if they did not
take a stand on the UNSCOP plan, Washington would be accused of
"pussyfooting," but adoption would mean violent Arab reaction and
a possible Soviet-Arab reproachment, and commitment to partition
would obligate the United States to take part in carrying it out.
Marshall spoke cautiously before the General Assembly on
September 17, saying that the United States gave weight to
recommendations approved by UNSCOP's majority report, but final
decision should be delayed until the plan was considered.[14]

The problem in the UNSCOP report for Washington was to
enforce the proposed plan, and the State Department suggested
looking at the possibility of drastically reducing the two-year
transition. The new ambassador Lewis W. Douglas in London, was
instructed to ask Bevin how Britain would view ending the mandate
on July 1, 1948, and working with a General Assembly commission
entrusted with the transfer of power to the two new states. The
Department was interested in what sort of assistance London was
prepared to offer. Douglas reported that he had spoken to Bevin

for more than an hour, and the usually voluble, indeed almost excitable, foreign secretary had refused to give any sign that the British government would cooperate in the transition.[15]

Events moved towards a solution, although the movement was not always clear to observers. It became apparent that the problem was what government (presumably the United States, which had decided to support partition) was going to stand behind any U.N. resolution. If no outside force was used in Palestine, and this solution seemed ever more likely, the local antagonists could solve their problems--and that would throw the arrangement into the hands of the Jewish Agency, whose forces were likely more ready for the violence than were the Arabs. The General Assembly on November 29, 1947, in a two-thirds vote, with the British government abstaining, supported partition.

Jewish Palestine was overjoyed when the U.N. voted for partition. Dancing, singing, cheering crowds filled the streets. Bands played until sunrise, and even British soldiers were warmly greeted. Chief Rabbi Isaac Herzog said: "After a darkness of two thousand years the dawn of redemption has broken."[16] In Jewish communities all over the world, especially in the United States, there was an outpouring of emotion together with pledges of support for the state.

Arab Palestine was outraged by the decision. The Arab Higher Committee announced rejection, called a three-day strike, and declared a boycott of Jewish enterprises. A manifesto proclaimed: "Palestine is our dear land. We were born in it. We have lived in it. We shall die in it. We shall then meet the

face of Allah with smiles, warm hearts, and satisfied souls."[17]
Throughout the Arab world there were demonstrations. In Damascus
crowds stoned the American legation, and in Cairo students broke
the windows of both British-owned and Jewish-owned stores.

Fighting between Arabs and Jews increased. The British
appeared unwilling or unable to keep the peace. Slowly the two
communities took control of their enclaves. A correspondent in
Jerusalem talked about events of December 20, a typical day: a
British soldier was shot in Tel Aviv, an Arab killed near
Jerusalem, two Jews wounded on the border between Tel Aviv and
Jaffa. He said it was madness for anyone without Arabic to enter
an Arab village, and suicide to do so in a beard, black hat, or
anything suggesting Jewish origin. The followers of the Mufti
were eliminating the last traces of moderation. Two Arabs had
been stoned to death for collaborating with the Jews. As
Britain's last Christmas in the Holy Land approached the road to
Bethlehem was a place of violence. There was no peace, no
goodwill.[18]

It appeared that some officials in the State Department were
having second thoughts about partition. The officials hinted to
their British counterparts that American support for partition
was waning. The Foreign Office reaction was simple: Washington
was responsible for the U.N. decision of November 1947--a
decision that London had refused to support--and now that an
American about-face appeared possible the British only wanted out
of Palestine. Instructing its U.N. delegation the Foreign Office
said that it should do nothing to oppose any American initiative

but should guard against giving the impression Britain would stay
in Palestine.[19]

One awkwardness led to another, for after the General
Assembly vote a five-member commission was appointed to carry out
partition. The Arab Higher Committee sent the U.N. Secretary
General what it called a declaration of war against partition,
saying the Arabs would fight to the last man. Concerned about
the safety of the commission after it arrived in Palestine,
Washington told London that the United States wanted the
commission to have every opportunity. Ignoring the American
position as well as U.N. directives the British government
refused to admit the full commission into Palestine until just
prior to the end of the mandate, but at the beginning of March
allowed an advance group to go to Palestine. The assistant
principal secretary of the commission, Pablo De Azcarate, later
wrote that this group realized that transfer of power from the
mandatory to the commission was of no significance because
British power in Palestine was diminishing, and the country was
divided.[20]

Zionists pressed President Truman to stand for partition.
At a staff meeting in the middle of February, Clark Clifford told
the president that some people blamed the American government for
inaction. Truman said he had done everything except mobilize
troops, that efforts were being made to induce Britain to keep
the peace, and he had "gone pretty far toward threatening Ernest
Bevin."[21]

Events in Europe cast a further shadow on partition; the

Soviet coup in Czechoslovakia early in 1948 shocked the West and
strengthened State Department officials who opposed the U.N.
decision. Ambassador Austin delivered a speech to the Security
Council in which he gave the first public indication that the
United States no longer supported partition. Colonial Secretary
Arthur Creech Jones present at the U.N., reported to the Foreign
Office that the speech had been drafted on the basis of
instructions received after a conversation between Truman and
Secretary Marshall. Pointing out that Britain had to preserve
its impartial attitude and not become involved in the situation
in the Security Council--a situation created by the United
States--he underlined the difficulties in any effort to bring the
Arabs and Jews together and said that the Soviet Union, which
supported partition, might reject conciliation.[22]

In the middle of March it appeared that there was
possibility of a confrontation with the Soviet Union. The
Soviets were unhappy about the American program for European
recovery, known as the Marshall plan, and there was mounting
disagreement over treatment of Germany. The London Conference of
Foreign Ministers, which had concluded its meetings in December
1947, had failed to settle differences. Afterwards the Western
powers made plans to integrate their zones of Berlin, form a West
German government, and provide for German participation in the
Marshall plan. As Churchill had declared two years before in his
iron curtain speech, the world was divided. The Communist coup
in Czechoslovakia seemed proof that the Soviet Union was moving
forward with a program of world conquest. The director of army

intelligence in Washington received an alarming telegram from the commander in Berlin, General Lucius D. Clay, that he had no evidence upon which to base his opinion but felt that at any time war was possible.[23]

No one was more suspicious of Soviet intentions than Foreign Secretary Bevin, who had proposed a Western Union, an alliance between Britain, France, Belgium, the Netherlands and Luxembourg, that could later be enlarged. With the blessing of the United States on March 17, 1948, the Brussels Pact--a fifty-year collective defense treaty--was signed. On the same day President Truman spoke to a joint session of Congress. The year before he had announced the Truman Doctrine--a global pledge to resist communist expansion. Pointing to the danger presented by the Soviet Union, he asked in 1948 for the immediate passage of the Marshall Plan, adoption of universal military training, and revival of the draft: "Our armed forces lack the necessary men to maintain their authorized strength."[24]

Difficulties with the Russians increased, and Soviet representatives on the Allied Control Council walked out of a meeting marking the breakdown of four-power government in Germany. Later the Soviets informed General Clay that their guard would check Americans passing through the Soviet zone en route to Berlin. There was no confrontation, but Clay told Washington that conditions would deteriorate when the United States moved forward with plans for rebuilding Germany.[25]

During these confusions the Palestine problem had to be delayed. Secretary of Defense James Forrestal wrote in his diary

at the beginning of March 1948 that people wanted the United
States to carry out the U.N. partition plan, but did not realize
that "the deployable army troops left in this country total less
than 30,000, to which might be added 23,000 marines, whereas the
British had to employ 90,000 troops merely to police the
Palestine area."[26]

The Soviet threat to Europe convinced the State Department
that partition had to be abandoned, and Austin on March 19 asked
the Security Council for a temporary trusteeship to maintain
peace and allow Arabs and Jews an opportunity to reach agreement.
Here was a move of policy that however logical to the State
Department did not have sufficient preparation. The president's
assistant press secretary Eben A. Ayers wrote in his diary that
March 20 was a bad day because hundreds of telegrams came into
the White House charging Truman with betrayal. At the morning
staff meeting the president said he had no idea that Ambassador
Austin planned to announce such a change in the American
position. Austin told Truman that his instructions came from the
State Department. According to Ayers' diary the president's
statement that Austin spoke without his knowledge seemed
"incredible and everyone looked glum and depressed." Clifford
attended the staff meeting and said that Secretary Marshall must
have known about the proposed speech. Truman told Clifford he
was wrong, because Marshall would never have ordered a shift in
policy without discussing it. Ayers could not understand how the
people involved ignored the political effect.[27]

The year 1948 was scheduled for a presidential election, and

Truman was fighting for his political life. He wrote in his memoirs that as leader of his party a president is in a position to control the nomination. Pointing out that in 1912 even the popular Theodore Roosevelt could not take the nomination from President Taft, he said that when he made up his mind to run, those who had turned against him could not prevent his nomination.[28] But in 1948 it was not clear that things would work out that way, or that after being nominated Truman would win. In the congressional elections of 1946 Republicans had won a large majority, enabling them for the first time since 1928 to take control of both houses of Congress. The Democratic party was so demoralized that Senator J. William Fulbright suggested that Truman resign so as to prevent a deadlock between a Democratic executive and a Republican legislature.[29] By July 1947 polls were showing gains for the president and in the early autumn he began considering strategy for the 1948 campaign. The president used his 1948 State of the Union address to open his campaign. Unwittingly he touched an exposed nerve of the South by speaking about essential human rights of all citizens and promising a special message to Congress. At the Jefferson-Jackson Day dinner in Little Rock, Arkansas, it was decided that instead of sending the money raised to the Democratic National Committee, the funds would be retained in Arkansas as a protest against the president's stand on civil rights.[30] Later the States Rights Party appeared, known as the Dixiecrats. That was not Truman's only worry, as former Vice President Henry A. Wallace, who had been fired as Secretary of Commerce for speaking out against the administration's foreign policy, said he feared

the president was leading the country into war with the Soviet

Union and had declared in December 1947 that he was running for

president as a third-party candidate. Then in March 1948 the

Americans for Democratic Action decided that to save the

Democratic party Truman would have to retire. It appeared that

the person with the prestige to win the election on the

Democratic party ticket was General Dwight D. Eisenhower.

Although Eisenhower showed no interest in the nomination,

Franklin D. Roosevelt Jr. and other liberals called on the party

to draft Ike.[31]

When the Foreign Office asked its Washington embassy for an

appraisal of the reasons why the United States adopted a new

position on Palestine, Lord Inverchapel referred to Truman's

political problems. He said the Zionists could be conciliated

only at the price of losing a great many voters who would react

against shedding blood in a Jewish cause. The Truman

administration could not hope to profit from the situation unless

it demonstrated singleminded devotion to the national interest.

It was an unusually complicated domestic situation. Truman,

Inverchapel said, may have lost patience with the Palestine

situation. Out of weakness the administration had perhaps

derived a newfound independence and sought to relieve its

embarrassment at Britain's expense.[32]

Unmoved by Truman's problems London stood on its decision to

withdraw from Palestine by the middle of May. One Foreign Office

official called the Arabs volatile, quarrelsome, undisciplined,

in love with money, but said geography and geology favored them.
Britain had an interest either in dominating the Arabs or
maintaining their friendship. Since domination was no longer
possible, friendship was essential. He warned that until the
problem was solved Palestine would hinder Anglo-Arab
friendship.[33] London told its U.N. delegation to abstain from
any public position, even if that meant refusal to support truce
proposals, a trusteeship, or a call for another special session
of the General Assembly. Pointing to opinion in the House of
Commons that the new American move was concerted with the British
government London warned that any support given Austin would
support that suspicion. Moreover, support for a truce might make
it difficult to resist appeals to leave troops in Palestine as
the instrument for maintaining that truce, and support for
trusteeship would be interpreted as a vote against partition--a
departure from Britain's position of neutrality.[34]

It had been concern with Soviet activity rather than
domestic politics that moved the American government away from
partition, and at the end of March it appeared that Washington
again might be changing policy. Now it was indeed politics.
Ayers wrote in his diary on March 24 that opposition to Truman's
nomination was spreading and that his shift on Palestine was a
factor. The following day before an unusually large crowd of
reporters--more than 150--the president read a statement on
Palestine, that the United States supported the partition plan
recommended by UNSCOP, but unfortunately the plan could not be
carried out without using force. The United States therefore

proposed a temporary trusteeship, which was not to become a substitute for partition but was a stop-gap.[35] Soon after Henderson gave the British embassy two drafts for a trusteeship agreement saying that American concern was a truce in Palestine-- essential to progress. The American government wanted both countries to issue an immediate appeal to the Arabs and Jews to stop fighting, but Henderson said he was not optimistic about the effectiveness of such an appeal because he doubted either side would commit itself as the eventual political solution remained unclear. Truman's statement to the press did not represent a change in policy. Reminding the British that nearly half of the Democratic party's funds came from Jewish sources, Henderson explained that although the president favored partition he was not going to exercise his influence to bring it into effect, despite pressure from members of Congress and others.[36]

If the United States was not going to support partition, how would the U.N. decision be enforced? It seemed in the spring of 1948 that the plan accepted by a two-thirds majority of the General Assembly, was doomed. Britain was not going to remain in Palestine, and no other nation or group of nations was willing to help.

CHAPTER 5

THE JEWISH STATE

Jews were angried by the retreat from partition; the
Zionists had no intention of foregoing a Jewish state, and in
Palestine the Jewish Agency Executive issued a statement that it
was astonished by the American attitude and that upon termination
of the mandate, no later than May 16, 1948, a provisional
government would begin to function. The chairman of the
executive, Ben-Gurion said the United States had surrendered to
terrorists armed by Britain. Shertock, on a fund-raising tour,
told a rally in Indianapolis that the United States had abdicated
its responsibility. He called Washington's new policy a Munich-
type appeasement. Secretary Marshall invited Shertock and his
colleague Epstein to the State Department to explain the change
in policy. He was told that the Agency would not agree to a
truce until all the Arab troops withdrew, and that while the
Agency had been willing to accept a British presence it no longer
would do so, nor would it accept trusteeship.[1] An editorial in
the Manchester Guardian underlined one of the most unfortunate
aspects of the situation by saying that the Jews would see
evidence that they were always persecuted: "It will fatten the
neurosis which already torments the Jewish people and blinds
their judgement."[2]

At the end of March Ambassador Austin moved two resolutions
in the Security Council: one called for an immediate truce, the
other asked for a special session of the Assembly. For the

second time all members of the world organization met to take up

Palestine. Washington asked the Foreign Office to help out, and

the American embassy in London presented an aide memoire on April

13, asking agreement on diplomatic and other means to obtain a

truce in concert with the United States, a possible partnership

with the United States and France in presentation of a

trusteeship plan to the General Assembly, and acceptance of

responsibility together with the United States and France for

security in Palestine. According to the aide memoire failure to

take action would impair the prestige of the U.N. and Britain

would appear responsible if the fighting resulted in Soviet

exploitation of either side.[3]

Bevin told Douglas that if the aide memoire became public it

would arouse such hostility that it might prove an opening for

communist propaganda. He said the American government should not

expect a reply. The State Department instructed Douglas to

emphasize joint action within the U.N. Douglas warned that a

noncommittal attitude would result in a situation dangerous to

world peace and made clear that talks with congressional leaders

left no doubt harm would result to every aspect of Anglo-American

interests if London refused to cooperate. Douglas reported that

Bevin did not want to be considered uncooperative but was at his

wits' end. Later he said Bevin talked to Attlee and other

colleagues and wanted Washington to know that the British

attitude was not inspired by unwillingness to cooperate but by

concern for British interests in the Arab world.[4]

As the United States tried to convince Britain to remain in

Palestine, events in that country moved towards a Jewish state.
It was estimated that about 7,000 volunteers, known as the army
of deliverance, entered Palestine under the command of Kawzi al
Kawukji who had been one of the leaders of the 1936 Arab revolt.
The Arab press had treated his defeats as victories and he
emerged as a hero. During World War II he went with the Mufti
to Iraq where in 1941 he participated in the pro-Axis coup
d'etat. When Fawzi entered Palestine in 1948 he brought no
medical supplies claiming that the campaign against the Jews
would be short, and without serious casualties. At the beginning
of April Kawukji led 1,500 men against the settlement of Mishmar
Haemek. Haganah offered strong resistance and the Arabs
withdrew, leaving thirty-eight dead clothed in Syrian and Iraqi
uniforms. Later Kawukji bragged that he took Mishmar Haemek in
ninety minutes and to find out how long it would take him to
conquer the Jews one would only have to multiply the number of
their settlements by ninety.[5]

Members of the Haganah displayed their elan at the end of
April: before being forced out by the British, who wanted
control of the area to secure their departure, the Jewish forces
seized a stronghold of Arab resistance, the Sheikh Jarrah quarter
in Jerusalem, and hoisted the blue and white Jewish flag--soon to
become the Israeli flag--over the mufti's house. Jerusalem's
Arabs, fearful of what would happen after the British departure,
piled their goods into every type of conveyance from limousine
to donkey cart and streamed out of the city toward Jericho and
Amman. Arab guards attempted to check the exodus, or to turn

back men of military age, but failed. When the British withdrew
from the city of Haifa into the port area the Haganah replaced
the departing troops and once in control issued a radio appeal
telling Jews to respect Arab property. Nevertheless only 800
Arabs applied to the Jewish administration for identity cards;
more than 35,000 Arabs fled the city. It was estimated that
before the beginning of May frightened Palestinian Arabs had
evacuated about thirty villages in the area of the proposed
Jewish state. Before the end of the mandate the Jews hence held
their ground and expanded control, leaving fewer Arabs in what
would become the Jewish state. A British Zionist who visited
Palestine reported to friends at home that "the temper of the
Jews in Palestine can be compared to Britain in the year when she
stood alone, determined to achieve victory and confident in the
ultimate result."[6]

During the last week in April 1948 the State Department
received information that King Abdullah had ordered an invasion
of Palestine. Marshall instructed Douglas to inform the British
that if any state sent forces into Palestine the United States
would have to take a stand in the U.N. Such a situation would
give the Soviets opportunity to send troops, a development that
would nullify efforts of Washington and London. Douglas spoke
to Attlee and Bevin and Attlee said it was unjust to expect
Abdullah to take no action, and Bevin offered a diatribe about
the Jewish position, remarking that American policy allowed Jews
to crush Arabs but did not want Arab countries to assist Arabs.
Douglas inquired about Abdullah's exact position and was told he

had not invaded Palestine. Yes, the Arab Legion under British command dug trenches on the Palestine side of the Allenby Bridge, but only to cover its retirement. Describing Palestine as an Arab country, Bevin said that there were few Arab infiltrators and their acts were exaggerated by arrogant Jews. Attlee asked why it was aggression for the Arabs to come to Palestine from neighboring countries but not aggression for European Jews to enter illegally. Douglas remarked mildly that Jewish immigrants entered unarmed as settlers not soldiers. Attlee said that was Hitler's method--put people in as tourists and arm them.[7]

Intent on ending the mandate, British leaders allowed the situation to drift, and at the beginning of May, Beeley traveled to Washington and in a Sunday morning conversation with Henderson said it was too late for trusteeship because of Jewish opposition--no Western power would use force. Although Britain was willing to do everything possible to arrange a truce, chances were poor. Usually sympathetic, Henderson told Beeley that Britain was responsible for the awful situation in Palestine because most American suggestions had been greeted in London by reticence.[8]

Suddenly the United States stopped pressing for British cooperation and Clifford brought up the Palestine problem at a staff meeting on May 8, Truman's sixty-fourth birthday; referring to the State Department's truce proposals as "love's labor lost" he said there was no possibility of a truce and the Department knew it.[9] As the date for the end of the mandate approached, Douglas reported to the State Department that the British did not find the situation as bad as expected. Considering Abdullah a positive factor, the Foreign Office was satisfied he would occupy Arab Palestine but refrain from attacking the Jewish state. With Arab Palestine under his control, according to London, a truce would be possible.[10]

At the special session of the General Assembly it was clear that the forty-seven-point plan for trusteeship put forward by Ambassador Austin failed to arouse the enthusiasm of the delegates, and it appeared unlikely that the American proposal would receive the necessary two-thirds majority. The representative of New Zealand said that the U.N. was forfeiting public confidence by going back on its own decision. Ambassador Gromyko announced that the Soviet Union would not vote for trusteeship and wanted to get on with partition. Three days before the scheduled date for the end of the mandate, on May 11, at a meeting of the subcommittee of the Assembly's Political and Security Committee, the Norwegian delegate, Finn Moe, said that it would be "ludicrous" if the mandate ended while the committee was still debating what to do.[11]

Fighting in Palestine intensified during the final days of the mandate as the British remained aloof. Jerusalem had been cut off from Tel Aviv for more than two weeks, but on May 10, after fierce fighting, the Haganah reopened the road. At the same time the Northern city of Safed fell to the Jews. Two days later it was clear that Jaffa, a city of 70,000 Arabs, which the partition plan had allotted to the Arabs, would go to the Jews. During the fighting the population fled, leaving Persian carpets, household goods, and well-stocked pantries. As the U.N. continued to debate, British forces stepped up preparations for departure, leaving the Arabs and the Jews to fight it out, to settle the question of Palestine as it had been settled over and over again for thousands of years.

With a sense of relief and with the hope that somehow or other things would work out, the British government ended thirty years in Palestine. The High Commissioner, Sir Alan Cunningham, on May 14 left his Jerusalem residence in a bullet-proof Daimler that had been loaned to him by his King. He was flown to Haifa. At the port an honor guard of the King's Company of Grenadier Guards and Royal Marine Commandos stood at attention as Cunningham, wearing the uniform of an army general, got into a launch that took him to to the cruiser Euryalus. At midnight after the British flag was lowered, rockets were fired, and the Euryalus set sail.

Announcement of the Jewish state was made on the afternoon of the High Commissioner's departure when Prime Minister of the Provisional Government of Israel David Ben-Gurion read the Declaration of Independence; members of the Jewish National Council of Palestine usually met in Jerusalem, but because the Holy City was under seige the historic session took place during modest ceremonies in an exhibition gallery of the Tel Aviv Museum of Art. Thirteen ministers of the governing council sat at a dais beneath a photograph of the founder of modern Zionism Theodore Herzl. The assembled crowd--approximately one hundred people--rose for the singing of Hatikvah. Celebrations were

muted: it was the eve of the sabbath and the country was at war.
But the citizens of the new state were confident; they were
determined to defend their freedom and at the same time to
welcome home their people still refugees in DP camps. The first
action of the government was to revoke the hated White Paper of
1939.

The United States moved back to partition. President Truman
was under tremendous pressure to recognize the Provisional
Government of Israel, known as PGI, and he granted de facto
recognition without even notifying Ambassador Austin at the U.N.,
where the special session was still considering the future of
Palestine. In his memoirs Truman said that partition did not
take place in the peaceful manner he had hoped, "but the fact was
that the Jews were controlling the area in which their people
lived and that they were ready to administer and to defend it."[12]
Reasons have been put forward to explain Truman's precipitate
action: the Jewish vote, importance of preempting the Soviet
Union, sympathy for the Jews. There is evidence to support all
of them. But in addition it is clear that recognition of the
Jewish state was an admission of failure: Truman and the State
Department had failed to keep the British in Palestine.

Distressed by the president's recognition of the Jewish
state London told its Washington embassy that Britain did not
want to drift away from the United States, but that the British
government had no intention of recognizing the PGI. Hence the
Foreign Office told the State Department that it would continue
military assistance to the Arab states until the U.N. ruled such

action contrary to Britain's obligation under the charter.
American policy placed a heavy strain on Anglo-American
cooperation in the Middle East, and according to Bevin unless it
was possible to induce the Arab states to retain confidence in
the friendly understanding of London and Washington on Palestine,
these countries would turn from the West.[13]

The situation changed in June; the Palestine problem paled
when, as General Clay had predicted, tension rose in Germany
between the Soviet Union and the West. After the United States
notified Moscow that the Reichmark would be replaced by the
Deutschmark, the Soviets determined to resist and set up the
blockade of Berlin. Truman responded with an airlift; American
and British planes carried supplies into West Berlin. Douglas
reported a change in British thinking; in the Foreign Office--
even among Arabists--was a conviction that the small sovereign
Jewish state was in the best interests of the Arabs.[14] Secretary
Marshall cabled Douglas at the end of June that he hoped the two
governments would now be able to work together and, keeping the
American commitment to Israel in mind, solve the problem.[15]

Concern over harmony with the United States in light of the
Berlin crisis did not mean London was ready to grant recognition
to the Jewish state; the British government wanted something done
for the Arab refugees who had fled their homes inside Israel.
There were conflicting reports about why the Arabs left. The
Arabs claimed that they were forced out by Jewish terror; the
Jews claimed that the Arab states had broadcast warnings telling
Arabs to leave, but promising that they would be able to return

with the victorious troops and inherit Jewish property. There
was certainty about the terrible conditions of the refugees. An
average daily ration made up exclusively of bread, was six
hundred calories. The U.N.-appointed mediator, Count Folke
Bernadotte, asked for American donations of wheat, canned meat,
cheese, butter, and DDT. While willing to help out with relief
supplies, the State Department agreed with the Foreign Office
that a permanent solution was needed, and that the best plan was
to return at least a portion of the refugees to their former
places inside Israel. Lovett talked to the special
representative of the PGI, Epstein, who said that Jewish
immigrants entering Israel had already settled in Arab houses,
and that returning Arabs would drain resources, endanger Israel's
security, and give up a bargaining point in peace negotiations.[16]
The American government pressed Israel to take back the refugees,
without success.

There was also the problem of boundaries for the Jewish
State. After proclamation of Israel the troops of five Arab
states, including Transjordan, invaded. The British officer who
served as commander of Abdullah's Arab Legion, Sir John Glubb,
said in his memoirs that the King had not wanted war with the
Jews but the other Arab states had insisted. According to Glubb
his troops were happy to go to war: military vehicles were
decorated with branches and flowers. In every village along the
route from Amman to the Allenby Bridge, cheering men lined the
road and the shrill cries of women and children could be heard
coming from windows and roof tops: "The procession seemed more

like a carnival than an army going to war." The Legion expected
to be in Tel Aviv within a few days.[17] The Security Council on
May 20 called on all of the warring parties to stop fighting.
Bernadotte arranged for a cease-fire that on June 11 went into
effect for four weeks. Although short of weapons the Haganah,
now the Israeli army, had been able to hold all of the land
assigned to the Jewish state as well as some of the territory
designated for the Arab state. Arab leaders continued to boast
that the Jews would be thrown into the sea but only the Legion
had achieved a meaningful victory, capturing the Jewish quarter
of the Old City of Jerusalem.

On the eve of the Arab invasion even the realistic Abdullah
had publicly proclaimed that Israel would be liquidated within
ten days and throughout the initial period of hostilities,
establishing a pattern that remains in force, the Arab press
published stories of glorious victories saying that the Jews were
on the verge of defeat. In a report on the BBC the journalist
Jon Kimche said that he was in a Galilee settlement drinking tea
with a group of farmers who were listening to an Arabic broadcast
from Damascus reporting the capture of that very settlement and
announcing hundreds of Jewish casualties.[18]

Despite their poor showing members of the Arab League were
determined to continue fighting. Abdullah said he entered the
fight half-heartedly but was eager to continue until the finish
and an Iraqi leader said that although some defeats were expected
the Arabs would ultimately prevail.[19] As the date for expiration
of the cease-fire approached the Security Council called for its

renewal and the British government applied strong pressure on all of the Arab states. The British minister in Amman warned Abdullah that since Britain had accepted a U.N. ban on arms shipments to the Middle East his Legion was short of ammunition. Suddenly frightened the King sent a letter by special plane to Cairo, where his prime minister was attending a meeting of the Political Committee of the Arab League, instructing him to veto renewal of hostilities. But the Political Committee had already voted unanimously to resume the war. Underlining that more fighting would be disastrous for the Arabs, British representatives in the Middle East urged that a new vote be taken but Arab leaders refused.[20]

The second round greatly improved the Jewish position. When the Egyptian army on July 8 opened fire in the South in an effort to gain control of the Negev, the Israelis, who had used the cease-fire period to train men and bring in arms, cut them off inflicting heavy casualties. The Israeli army also launched an offensive into Arab Palestine taking Lydda, Ramallah and Nazareth. Resistance in Lydda was strong. One hundred Arabs held out in a fortified police station. Seeing no possibility of victory the village mayor appealed to them to surrender. He was shot. The Security Council ordered a cease-fire on July 15 and the battered Arab states willingly agreed, but Israel now on the offensive only reluctantly complied.

Disgruntled the Arabs blamed Britain for their defeat saying London had pressed them to accept a truce when they were near victory. Bevin sent policy guidelines in August to all Middle

East posts explaining that the Attlee government had not let the Arabs down, had not urged intervention in Palestine, had not promised support. It was clear that the Arab states could not drive the Jews into the sea, and they had to face reality, assume responsibility. Arab governments deluded their people and now had to accept facts: refusal to follow British advice, to renew the truce, resulted in additional loss. The Palestine problem had to be settled and London would continue to try for settlement favorable to the Arabs, but the Arabs had to keep the peace because only the Jews would profit from resumption of fighting.[21]

From the period of the first cease-fire Bernadotte worked on proposals for solution. He did not consider himself bound by the boundaries of the U.N. plan and put forward a plan that would assign western Galilee to the Jews and the Negev to the Arabs. Ben-Gurion's government was willing to accept western Galilee, which Israel had already occupied, but the Jews would not agree to removal of the Negev from the Jewish state--the Negev had been given to Israel because of Weizmann's intercession with President Truman. Bevin liked the Bernadotte plan and was especially interested in the proposal to give the Negev to the Arabs. Soon after the first cease-fire Beeley told members of the American U.N. delegation that he did not understand why the Jews were so keen on that waterless territory.[22] Special Assistant to the Director of the Office of U.N. Affairs Robert McClintock, who shared in the formulation of American Palestine policy, later said that the British government "developed a passionate strategic interest in this stony and arid desert." Generals

and diplomats told Ambassador Douglas that the links of empire
would crumble if Britain's Arab allies did not have this
territory on which to build airfields, and that a direct line of
communications between Egypt and Transjordan was essential if a
defense line against Russia across Northern Syria was to hold.[23]

At first the State Department was uncertain about how to
respond to the Bernadotte plan. Before leaving on vacation
McClintock wrote to his boss, the Director of the Office of U.N.
Affairs Dean Rusk, saying he was going to Martha's Vineyard "to
wash away the sins of the Chosen People--and their equally sinful
adversaries--in clear salt water."[24] After McClintock returned
from vacation the American position moved closer to Britain's.
Marshall in the middle of August sent a memorandum to the
president complaining about Israel, pointing to evidence of
Israeli hostility toward the military observers serving under
Bernadotte, Israeli truce violations, and shipment of arms from
Czechoslovakia into Israel. He said that Bevin was concerned
about Israeli aggression--Bevin had called the Palestine
situation as serious as the Berlin crisis.[25] Bevin wanted
American support for the Bernadotte plan, and said that it was
important for all proposals to be labeled "mediator-made in
Sweden" because if a plan appeared to be the product of Anglo-
American cooperation the Arabs would resist.[26]

Washington agreed at the beginning of September to send
McClintock to Bernadotte's headquarters in Rhodes to meet with
the mediator and Sir John Troutbeck of the Foreign Office in
order to go over Bernadotte's proposals. The State Department

told its embassy in London that the purpose of McClintock's visit to Rhodes had to remain secret and if questions were asked the embassy was to reply that McClintock was studying the refugee problem.[27] During discussions in Rhodes McClintock said that it would be wise to give Israel some sort of holding in the Negev. Nevertheless, he agreed to recommend American support. Pleased that there was now Anglo-American unity Bevin gave Douglas a draft of a statement he proposed to make in support of the Bernadotte plan saying that it had been written with trepidation because it put Britain on record as favoring partition.[28]

Bernadotte presented what was to be his last report to the U.N. on September 16 saying that the Jewish state envisioned in the partition plan had been established, but that in the portion of Palestine under Arab control no central authority existed and that there was no Arab state. It appeared impossible to set up an independent Arab state, so the governments of the Arab states ought to consult and decide what to do with that territory. His view was that because of the historical connection and common interests of Transjordan and Palestine, there would be compelling reasons for merging the Arab territory of Palestine with Transjordan. Bernadotte also said that the Galilee should be defined as a Jewish area, the Negev should be defined as an Arab area, and the towns of Ramallah and Lydda--taken by the Jews after the expiration of the first cease-fire--should be returned to the Arabs.[29]

Terrorists struck; while driving through the Israeli-held section of Jerusalem on September 17, Bernadotte was

assassinated. He had served as president of the Swedish Red
Cross, had intervened with the Nazis near the end of the war, and
was credited with rescue of concentration camp inmates, but his
record as a humanitarian did not impress the Jewish extremists.
Months before the assassination he had received death threats,
and in the weeks preceding his murder posters appeared showing
him being kicked out of Israel with a huge boot.[30]

Bevin wanted the Bernadotte plan to become a monument to the
martyred U.N. mediator, and the Foreign Office told the State
Department that Bernadotte's death underlined the need for
action, that support for the plan should continue. The American
government agreed. There was statement making by both Britain
and the United States in support of the late mediator's
proposals.

The assassination did not turn the Truman administration
from the Bernadotte plan, but with the presidential election
approaching political considerations prevailed. Secretary
Marshall was in Paris attending a session of the General
Assembly, and he told the Assembly that the United States
supported the Bernadotte plan as a basis for negotiations. The
Cambridge-educated Israeli diplomat, Abba Eban, wrote later that
American support for the plan was disconcerting: "It was vital
for us to detach the United States from the Bernadotte plan, and
this involved me in heavy lobbying with the United States
delegation."[31] President Weizmann sent a cable to Truman's
former business partner Eddie Jacobson asking him to use his
influence with the president.[32] The Democratic party platform

had endorsed the Israeli boundaries designated in the partition
resolution and some democrats warned that Marshall's statement
in Paris had harmed the president politically. Truman did not
immediately respond. There had been an informal understanding
between the two major parties that they would not make political
issue out of foreign policy, and Truman did not want to say
anything that would give the impression he was breaking the
agreement. Unwittingly the Republicans helped the president.
Dewey's candidate for secretary of state, John Foster Dulles,
was a member of the American U.N. delegation in Paris, and had
withheld support for Marshall's acceptance of the Bernadotte
plan. Eban wrote that Dulles' Protestant mysticism led him to
give the question of Israel "a larger importance than its
geopolitical weight would indicate." Dulles was certain Dewey
would be elected, so sure that he had invited several U.N.
representatives to a dinner party scheduled for the evening after
victory.[33] Then Dewey released a private letter in which he
attacked the president's Palestine policy, saying he supported
the boundaries for Israel designated in the partition resolution.
Here was opportunity for Truman; aboard the presidential campaign
train Clifford called Secretary Lovett and told him Marshall had
overemphasized the Bernadotte plan. Lovett cabled the secretary
in Paris saying that Dewey had violated the bipartisan approach
to foreign policy and that the president had to affirm support
for the Democratic platform. In a statement on October 24,
Truman said he supported the platform on Palestine. Four days
later, six days before the election, speaking at Madison Square

Garden before an audience of sixteen thousand, Truman praised the Jewish pioneers who had created a modern state out of barren desert, talked about how much his administration had contributed to establishment of Israel, and while not mentioning the Bernadotte plan by name made clear that it did not have his support.[34]

After Truman's victory at the polls the British once more pressed for the Bernadotte plan. First Secretary at the London embassy, G. Lewis Jones, wrote to McClintock on November 16 saying that the British are "extremely jittery" because we have no instructions.[35] Then Bevin sent a personal message to Marshall underlining that Britain had announced support for the Bernadotte plan only after the United States had agreed to support those proposals--British policy was based on the assumption of a common stand.[36] London was disappointed, but the situation in Palestine had changed by the middle of November and the United States now wanted the Israelis to retain the Negev.

Despite the truce Israel had moved in October to force open the road to the Negev. Ben-Gurion told his government that even if the U.N. was not considering removal of the Negev from the Jewish state something would have had to be done to push back the Egyptians: "We would have to capture the road to the south if it were only because we have twenty-six settlements on the other side of the Egyptian lines."[37] The operation was set for October 14, the day after the Yom Kippur fast. Without giving any sort of explanation Chief Rabbi Herzog ruled that soldiers could work and eat on Yom Kippur. The Egyptians assisted the

Israelis by giving them a pretext for renewal of hostilities.

When the Egyptians fired on an Israeli convoy, which according

to the truce agreement should have been allowed to pass, the

Israeli army began "Operation Ten Plagues"; immediately the

entire air force went into action against Egyptian positions and

a general attack began. After seven days of fighting the PGI

finally accepted a cease-fire. Israel now controlled the

northern Negev. The Egyptians--about three battalions--were cut

off in Faluja without any means of supplying their troops.

The State Department told the Foreign Office that security

could not be found in any given line drawn in the desert or in

an effort to contain an embittered Israel behind a ring of weak

Arab states backed by British military supplies, that the best

assurance of Anglo-American interests would be a friendly

Israel.[38] Washington was committed to Israel.

Zionism had succeeded. There was a viable Jewish state in

Palestine. The PGI was able to administer its territory and the

Israeli army was able to defend that territory. The commander

of the battalion that had captured Lydda, Colonel Moshe Dayan,

said in the middle of December that Israel was in a fortunate

position "being willing and able to engage in both war or peace

talks."[39]

CHAPTER 6

ARAB PALESTINE

From the moment Abdullah became Emir of Transjordan in 1922
he wanted to enlarge his domain, regaining territory lost when
the French drove his brother Feisal from Syria and Ibn Saud drove
his father Hussein from the Hejaz. Transjordan had been part of
Palestine and Abdullah coveted territory there. During the
mandate the British viewed Transjordan and Palestine as an
entity. The British resident in Amman was subordinate to the
High Commissioner in Jerusalem, and Transjordan received revenue
from Palestine excises. While Transjordan was administered by
Britain the country could not expand, but Britain granted
independence in May 1946, and Abdullah assumed the title of king.
To celebrate the narrow streets of Amman were decorated with
flags and pictures of the monarch. A brief ceremony took place
in the palace throne room, and wearing a flowing black robe the
king was driven to the Legion parade grounds in a cream-colored
Daimler where Glubb Pasha joined him. A colorful parade passed
the reviewing stand including the camel corps, known as "Glubb's
Girls." Excluded from the festivities, Abdullah's three wives
watched from a nearby balcony. The first British Ambassador to
Transjordan, Sir Alec S. Kirkbride, who one reporter called "the
perennial Englishman, enormously tall and perfectly
imperturbable," had served in that country since 1921 and
developed friendship with the king.[1] Kirkbride reported to the
Foreign Office that as ruler of an independent state Abdullah had

lost his inferiority and planned to take part in Middle Eastern affairs. At the same time the king wanted harmony with Britain; he said other Arab states made pretentious claims to a freedom they were in no position to defend, but he understood the importance of friendship with Britain.[2] Hence before enlarging his kingdom Abdullah wanted approval.

Abdullah agonized over how to annex Arab Palestine without offending larger Arab states, and Kirkbride reported in October 1947 that the king was more unsettled than at any time in the twenty-seven years of their association: he worried about Arab reaction to a takeover of Arab Palestine, and wanted Foreign Office support, for a Jewish state would be difficult for Transjordan without the outlet to the Mediterranean afforded by Arab Palestine.[3] Kirkbride reminded London that strategically and economically Transjordan had the best claim, that if Abdullah took Arab Palestine he would agree to a Jewish state.[4]

Even after the U.N. voted partition, an independent Jewish state and an independent Arab state, the British government agreed that Arab Palestine should go to Transjordan. Here was one issue about which in May 1948 there appeared Anglo-Israeli agreement. The Zionist leader assigned to London, Nahum Goldmann, told Ambassador Douglas that "our relations with Abdullah have always been good and he would make the best possible neighbor for us." If Abdullah's troops marched into Palestine, according to Goldmann, the Jewish Agency would protest to the Security Council, but if they stopped at the Israeli frontier it would not be in the Jewish interest to brand

Transjordan an aggressor.[5]

The Arab Legion occupied Arab Palestine and King Abdullah together with his officers stood at the eastern end of the Allenby bridge on the evening of May 14, 1948, waiting expiration of the mandate. At midnight the king drew his revolver, fired a shot in the air, and shouted "forward."[6] But after suffering the loss of Ramleh and Lydda he decided against more hostilities. A noisy demonstration in front of the royal palace at the beginning of August 1948 demanded renewal, and the king descended from the palace steps and boxed the ears of one vocal critic and ordered the names of all demonstrators taken so they would be dispatched for immediate service at the front. There were no more demonstrations.[7]

The other Arab League states took steps to thwart him, and meeting in Alexandria the Political Committee of the Arab League passed a resolution proclaiming an Arab government for Palestine, with the mufti excluded from leadership.[8] Under Egyptian auspices a government calling itself the Government of All Palestine set itself up in Gaza. Trucks escorted by Egyptian troops arrived in Bethlehem carrying small arms, distributed to Palestinians opposed to Abdullah. Irregulars held courts of justice, levied taxes and recruits.[9] Meeting at the end of September a seventy-five-member National Council issued a declaration of independence, which defined the borders of the state as Syria and Lebanon in the north, Syria and Transjordan in the east, Mediterranean in the west, Egypt in the south. Partition called for an Arab state in Palestine, but the Gaza government claimed all Palestine and refused to recognize a Jewish state. It was clear that men involved in the new government belonged to the mufti.

Neither the British nor the Americans approved the Gaza government. London had encouraged an Arab League to promote coordination; now it considered the League an impediment to peace. The Foreign Office told the Egyptian government that Arabs were playing into the hands of Jews, an Arab claim to all Palestine would precipitate a Jewish counterclaim.[10] The Secretary General of the League, Azzam Pasha, insisted that the Government of All Palestine, approved by the League, was the only legal government, that the mufti's role was military--he commanded 2,000 holy warriors. Azzam agreed that the mufti was no good and explained that if the Palestine issue was settled "I would cut his throat," but that the problem would take years and the mufti, enemy of the Jews, was useful. Azzam admitted that some day partition might come, but there was no harm in the Gaza government.[11] After reading Azzam's comments Glubb wrote to the Foreign Office: "Azzam Pasha, the mufti, and the Syrian government would rather see the Jews get the whole of Palestine than that Abdullah should benefit."[12]

The Foreign Office asked representatives in Arab countries to do everything to prevent recognition of the Government of All Palestine, but to no avail. The Arabs were angry that the British government had not prevented a Jewish state, and now that the League was setting up an Arab state Arab leaders objected to Foreign Office interference. The Syrian minister of foreign affairs said only Palestinians in Amman opposed the Gaza government.[13]

Washington wanted to discourage recognition and told Arab governments that because the mufti was the force behind the Government of All Palestine no Western government would deal with Gaza, which would never achieve standing in the world community. Such a government would do the Palestinians no good. Deputy Foreign Minister Yusuf Yassin said to the American representative in Jidda that the State Department did not understand: the mufti was the real leader, but Palestinians wanted the mufti.[14]

Describing the mufti as "a devil straight from hell," Abdullah moved against the Gaza government and organized a meeting against the mufti in Amman at the beginning of October. A former Jaffa journalist, Suleiman Farouki, exhorted the crowd of about 2,500 to oppose the Gaza government. Pro-mufti demonstrations had taken place in Hebron and Bethlehem, and the mufti's followers organized several groups in Legion-held territory. Now the Legion sought to discover the ringleaders. Kirkbride was concerned that the situation might lead to civil war and said that "when they are not fighting someone else they fight each other."[15]

Arrival of the mufti in Gaza changed the situation, for Husseini was warmly received. The League agreed he was to stay out of Gaza. Angered by the mufti's independence, Farouk ordered his immediate return to Cairo and instructed the army to see to it.[16] Soon afterward the Gaza government asked the League for £20 million, and when the Israelis moved against the Egyptians in the middle of October the Government of All Palestine fled to Cairo.

At this juncture there were two possibilities in Arab Palestine: an independent state as called for in the partition plan, or union with Transjordan as suggested by the U.N. mediator. Because no Palestinian leader had appeared except the mufti, Abdullah's position was strong. An American official in the Middle East reported to the State Department that after realizing the Arab troops were not going to defeat the Jews many Palestinians once more had fallen under the mufti's spell, but an equal number supported Abdullah as an antidote for Husseini. Yet if it would be possible to hold a plebiscite in which all Palestinians could vote, there was no way of predicting how it would turn out.[17]

Britain favored giving Arab Palestine to Transjordan, and the government wanted the United States to agree. As a first step Amman needed American recognition. When Abdullah's kingdom became independent in 1946, Washington withheld recognition. Zionists insisted that the British government ignored Jewish interests in granting independence to Transjordan. The embassy in Washington explained to the Foreign Office that the Jews would seek to prevent recognition until the Palestine problem was solved.[18] London told the State Department that clauses in the mandate relating to the Jewish national home never applied to Transjordan, that prior to independence the British government had not been under obligation to consult the Jewish Agency or secure Agency consent.[19]

After establishment of Israel, Transjordan pressed for
American recognition and the Jews withdrew objection. The
Transjordanian prime minister protested that friendship with
Amman was shunned, yet Israel was recognized in ten minutes.
Stressing that Britain, Transjordan, and the United States ought
to work together to fight communism, he offered to go to
Washington to clear up misunderstanding.[20] At the same time
Goldmann told Douglas that the Zionists now considered it in
Israel's interest to accord Abdullah prestige, and suggested
recognition might be a reward for an agreement with Israel, that
Washington should send an unofficial representative to Amman.[21]

The Arab Legion controlled Arab Palestine; hence Abdullah's
position was strong and his cooperation essential. The American
Consul in Jerusalem reported in June 1948 that Transjordan was
becoming a political and military center, that officers of the
Consulate General occasionally visited Amman, the British
sometimes made information available, but the situation was no
longer satisfactory, and because it was likely that influence and
strategic importance of Transjordan would increase it would be
wise to assign a consular officer to Amman.[22]

Washington moved towards recognition when at the beginning
of July a Foreign Service officer transferred from Jerusalem,
Wells Stabler, arrived in Amman. Abdullah was pleased. Yet a
great deal of information he reported to the State Department
came from the indispensable Kirkbride. Brought up in the Middle
East he was fluent in Arabic, knowledgeable about Islam, and had
contact with all factions. He spent at least one day weekly at

the palace--Shuneh during the summer, Amman the rest of the
year--and slept overnight, and was consulted on personal and
political matters and virtually became Abdullah's brother.

Secretary Marshall wanted to work out an arrangement whereby
the British government would extend recognition to Israel at the
same time the American government recognized Transjordan.
Marshall told Douglas that Abdullah had played a part in securing
Arab agreement to the second truce, had cooperated with the
mediator, and would continue to show moderation. In addition
Israel wanted the United States to recognize Transjordan. It
seemed best to grant recognition at the same time as de jure
recognition to Israel, after the Jewish state held its election
of a government to replace the PGI. According to Marshall de
jure recognition to Israel without recognition to Transjordan
would cause trouble. But American recognition to Transjordan
without British recognition to Israel would also be a problem.
The Anglo-Americans had to work out a solution and that was
impossible without cooperation of all parties. Marshall
instructed Douglas to talk to Bevin.[23]

Here was a problem for the British Cabinet, where there was
still a strong anti-Israel bias. The British remembered Jewish
terrorism, so recently directed against them. There also
remained an uncomfortable taste of failure: the state of Israel
stood as a monument to the defeat of London's Palestine policy.
Moreover, the Cabinet did not want to upset the Arabs. In
addition the Israelis appeared unwilling to let bygones be
bygones, underlined by treatment of the British consulate in

Haifa; the consulate had been burglarized, members of the staff harassed, consular mail censored. An Israeli official explained that such actions were not part of policy, but acts of overzealous junior officials who saw any Briton as a "potential enemy."[24]

In the almost constant maneuvers between Western capitals, London and Washington, and in the movements of opinion and guesswork between Tel Aviv and Amman and elsewhere within the Middle East, the talk of what might happen to Arab Palestine went on, and the inauguration of President Truman for a full term as president, elected in his own right, in January 1949, did not seem to mean much. With Truman's inaugural came a new secretary of state, Dean Acheson, who replaced the ailing Marshall, and that too did not augur anything for the Middle East. The principals in the negotiations locally over Arab Palestine--Tel Aviv and Amman--looked to their own concerns, and failed to realize that as advices passed from representatives of the United States and Britain there was not much conviction behind the words. The truth was that the Truman administration was concerned with other issues--at the moment its triumph over the Republican party in the person of Governor Thomas E. Dewey, but shortly after the ending of the Berlin blockade and in the autumn of 1949 there was the explosion, deep within the Soviet Union, of a nuclear device and the resultant decision, taken almost immediately by the administration, to go ahead with a hydrogen weapon. In London concerns were mainly economic, the slow upward movement of the British economy, thanks to infusions of assistance from the Marshall Plan, and all the while an acute feeling that the imperial concerns of earlier years, the grand domination from London of enormous areas and huge populations in the Far East and the Middle East, were no longer possible. Already in 1947 the British government had given India to the Indians, Greece and Turkey to the United States, and Palestine to the United Nations. And so when Kirkbride made comments to Abdullah the commentary was likely to be more personal than official, and when McDonald in Tel Aviv consulted the new Israeli leaders he too was speaking largely without government guidance. Both representatives--and the Arab monarch in Amman uneasily sensed this fact--were sometimes acting on their own.

Such were the governing realities. When Acheson took over the State Department, the British embassy in Washington reported that so far as concerned Arab Palestine the new secretary would press for a settlement just to have the problem settled. Time was against an equitable settlement. If London delayed Washington might force more concessions from the Arabs.[25] At a Cabinet meeting on January 17, 1949, the Minister of Health, Aneurin Bevan, said events in Palestine confirmed the wisdom of friendship with the Jews, that it was difficult to withhold de facto recognition. Ministers disagreed, saying commonwealth connections made it essential to support the Arabs, that before recognition several governments would have to be consulted.[26] Next day answering a question in the Commons, Bevin used the phrase "government of Israel," although before he had avoided reference to the Jewish state, instructing the Foreign Office to

refer to the PGI as "the Jewish authorities in Palestine." The
Foreign Office sent an urgent message to Washington, asking
Transjordan be immediately recognized, that the State Department
move before the Israeli elections because this would enable
Britain to recognize Israel and perhaps prevent demand for a
greater Israel. Before the Department replied the British backed
away. The Benelux governments told the Foreign Office they were
anxious for recognition simultaneously by the Western Union
governments, and the commonwealth countries continued to oppose
recognition.[27] The Commons on January 26, 1949, debated
Palestine policy and as usual Bevin implied that he alone
understood the issues and protected interests in the Arab world,
that the United States was responsible for all problems in the
Middle East. In top form Churchill said British policy was moved
by ill will, always behind events, passing from disaster to
disaster.[28]

The Cabinet decided recognition was inevitable, delay no
longer in Britain's interest. An election had been held in
Israel: 440,000 people went to the polls, a small showing for
Menachem Begin, victory for the moderate Mapai of David Ben-
Gurion. In granting de facto recognition the British stipulated
it did not affect Israel's frontiers.

Washington was pleased. Here was evidence that Britain was
once again willing to work for solution. It seemed at the time
that the Jews would have to compromise on frontiers and the Arabs
would have to accept the permanence of Israel. First Secretary
Jones at the London embassy wrote a friend at the State

Department that since May 14, 1948, his work had been to get London to catch up with Washington and it was only by restraint that after Britain announced recognition he refrained from sending the Department a one-word telegram, "Hurray!"[29]

Israel had British recognition, at least de facto, and at the beginning of February 1949 the United States extended de jure recognition both to Israel and Transjordan. It now seemed that the Palestine problem was going to be resolved. Abdullah could annex Arab Palestine. There remained the problem of Arab reaction, and something had to be done to arrange agreement with the Jewish state, for it would be dangerous to take Arab Palestine without Israeli cooperation.

Months before gaining recognition Abdullah had made up his mind to settle with Israel. Even before establishment of the Jewish state the king held conversations with the Jews. Chairwoman of the Jewish Agency's Political Department, the Russian-born, Milwaukee-educated Golda Meir, disguised in vail and Arab dress, traveled to Transjordan. Abdullah told her he would not attack the Jews. Later when it appeared that Transjordan was going to join the Arab League, Meir sent a message asking if the king had changed his mind. Abdullah replied he was hurt by the question, that he was a Bedouin and a king and therefore honorable, "and finally, that he would never break a promise made to a woman." So Meir returned to Amman and Abdullah sadly explained he was forced to break his promise, but following battle they would talk.[30] At the beginning of August 1948, Abdullah sent word to Shertock, who after becoming Israel's foreign minister took the Hebrew name Sharett, that he was willing to hold conversations in Paris. Delighted, the Israeli government sent agents. Now London told Abdullah that he was moving too quickly, that it was too early to detach himself from the Arab world, that it would encourage the Jews to think they could do well negotiating with him and they would resist a U.N.-arranged settlement.[31] The king's men did not go to Paris.

Abdullah was impatient. He had asked the United States to serve as intermediary with the Jewish state, but Washington was concerned that a settlement produce such an outcry the king might renounce it, and did not want to take action that could harm Anglo-American cooperation.[32] The Israeli government appeared well informed about most messages exchanged among the parties and at lunch on November 11, Prime Minister Ben-Gurion told the ardent Zionist McDonald that he did not understand American policy.[33]

Amman began negotiations with Tel Aviv. Contacts between Transjordan and Israel came to Kirkbride's attention when Abdullah's prime minister showed the British ambassador a message from the Transjordanian minister in London suggesting that since talks with Israel were going so well it would be a good idea to move discussion to Jerusalem.[34] Kirkbride was in a quandary. The Foreign Office did not like direct negotiations, preferring political talks between Transjordan and Israel under the aegis of the U.N. Palestine Conciliation Commission. But London also said it would be folly to tell Amman not to come to terms with Tel Aviv because understanding offered the only hope for peace.[35]

In January 1949 the British government seemed to approve of direct negotiations. Bevin told the Cabinet it offered the only way, opportunity to get the Arabs and Jews together. The day before the Cabinet meeting Eliyahu Sasson and Brigade Commander Dayan visited Abdullah. Sasson, born in Damascus, was the only Jewish member of the Arab Syrian National Committee, and after the First World War had greeted Abdullah's brother Feisal as King of Syria. Dayan was now living in the mansion of a wealthy Arab lawyer, Abkarius Bey, who had fled Jerusalem, and his family furnished their new house with items purchased from a warehouse managed by the Custodian of Enemy Property. Ruth Dayan later said that human nature is good at rationalization, that if the Dayans had not taken those things some other family would have.[36] It was clear the Israelis wanted peace, but that they were unwilling to give up what they had gained.

Meetings between Abdullah and the Israelis continued, and at the beginning of February, Transjordan agreed to attend talks under U.N. auspices in Rhodes. Kirkbride was concerned about American de jure recognition and British de facto recognition, that it had stiffened Israel, that the Israelis intended to keep Ramleh and Lydda, two towns from which Arabs were still leaving. Defense Minister Fawzi El Mulki said that if settlement was not reached quickly all Palestine would be in Jewish hands. Fearing a quick settlement as much as he feared a new round of hostilities Kirkbride persuaded the king to send a low-level delegation--three Legion officers--to Rhodes.[37]

The king told Stabler that before the Rhodes talks he

planned a meeting with the Israelis at Shuneh so they could come to terms privately. Abdullah underlined the importance of an outlet to the sea; he had considered Jaffa but dismissed it because of its location next to Tel Aviv, and now favored Gaza.[38] The king was talking settlement. The State Department was dismayed by Abdullah's interest in territorial questions. Officials agreed with their British counterparts that it was better to take first things first, that it would require a long time to agree on territory.[39] American pressure persuaded Abdullah to leave that question until after an armistice.

Before an armistice Israel wanted access to the Gulf of Akaba, and while Israeli and Transjordanian representatives were talking Israeli troops occupied it. Egypt, the first Arab state to sign an armistice with Israel, had been forced from its positions in the Negev at the beginning of January, and although the Egyptian press was still printing stories of glorious victories the Egyptians signed an armistice on February 24, 1949. Afterwards the Ben-Gurion government ordered occupation of the southern Negev, which according to the partition plan was Israeli. Stabler saw evidence of Israel's "perfidious intentions," recommending that the United States demand a return to positions held prior to the Rhodes talks.[40] He was ignored.

Tel Aviv said the Negev was Israeli territory, and according to Eban the Arab Legion was fifty miles north of Akaba and had as much right to lines there as to lines "in the middle of Broadway."[41] On the morning of March 10, 1949, the Israeli flag was raised over the Umm Reshresh police station on the shores of

the Gulf of Akaba west of the Transjordanian frontier. McDonald
said Israeli troops had not crossed the Egyptian or
Transjordanian frontiers. The Israeli government was aware of
Britain's treaty obligations to both countries and had no wish to
clash with Britain. One Israeli official remarked that "if there
is no respect for our integrity there should be some respect for
our intelligence."[42]

Abdullah was not concerned about Israeli occupation of the
Negev or about having the Jews in Akaba. But the British were
upset and Kirkbride responded in what unfortunately had become
Foreign Office talk, that Israeli moves bore a striking parallel
to Hitler's.[43] The British ambassador was convinced that the
Jewish state would take every opportunity to expand and that the
king should be careful. Abdullah was convinced the Israeli
government had no intentions towards his territory and remained
committed to a settlement. The talks in Rhodes continued.

Another problem arose in March when Abdullah wanted to
replace Iraqi troops with Legion troops. The Iraqis had fought
on the front lines, but did not desire an armistice with Israel
and the king wanted to consolidate control, easier if the Iraqis
went home, so Amman and Baghdad arranged to allow Iraqi troops to
pull out. Here was a pretext for Israel to make gains that would
produce more rational frontiers. Israeli soldiers moved into
positions opposite the Iraqis and the Hebrew press devoted space
to reported raids from Iraqi-held territory. Fearing a clash
with Israeli forces, Abdullah decided to postpone takeover of
Iraqi positions until he had Israeli approval.[44]

Bevin wanted the United States to deter Israel from taking more territory. He asked Ambassador Douglas to tell the Department that if the Jews confronted the world with another fait accompli achieved by military means it would damage the U.N. and turn the Arabs against the West. Complaining that despite the embargo, observed by Britain and the United States, Israel was getting arms, he said it was ridiculous for his government to refuse to rearm the Legion.[45] Douglas reported to Washington.

Meanwhile Dayan met Abdullah to tell him Israel needed territory but understood the king's political problems-- concessions would enrage the Arab states. According to Dayan, Tel Aviv required that the king sign an agreement not to go into effect for several months. Israeli agents went to Shuneh on the evening of March 23, exchanged greetings, sat down to a five-course dinner, and then presented their demands. According to the Foreign Office the Israelis "in manner reminiscent Hitler with late president Czechoslovakia" frightened and confused the king and succeeded in getting him to initial an agreement giving up sixty kilometers of land.[46] Dayan did not see any evidence that Abdullah was confused. After signing the agreement at three o'clock in the morning the Israelis presented the king with a silver-bound Bible from Ben-Gurion and the king gave the four Israelis gifts and roses. Before they left the palace Abdullah blessed them saying: "Tonight we have ended the war and brought peace."[47]

The State Department decided that because Abdullah had agreed to give up territory it was too late to approach Israel.

The king was not angry with Tel Aviv or Washington and told Stabler he had wanted peace negotiations in the summer of 1948, that if Britain had not interfered he would have obtained much better conditions. He said the British urged delay, confident of the Americans, but it was clear Britain was no longer capable of independent action, that Britain would have to follow the Americans.[48]

Israel and Transjordan on April 13, 1949, signed an armistice, which pleased the king and the Israelis. After friction at the opening session in Rhodes relations between the Israeli and Transjordanian delegates had been friendly. According to Dayan the Legion officers led by Ahmed Sudki el-Jundi "may well have been experts at maintaining order in Jordan and pursuing robber bands in the southern desert," but they did not know how to negotiate. It did not matter because the delegation was a facade; Abdullah secretly conducted negotiations. The Legion officers followed orders and if there was a garbled word in a cabled instruction they asked for adjournment.[49]

The Arab Palestinians opposed the armistice, resenting article six that required turning over sixteen villages in the Jenin-Nablus-Tulkarm triangle area to Israel. About 35,000 villagers protested that during the fighting they defended their homes, and saw no justification for surrendering land. Many said Abdullah had no right to speak for them, that the United States and Britain should have stood up to the Israelis. The clause turning over land to Israel stipulated that villagers were welcome to remain, and hoping to improve relations with the Arabs the Israelis encouraged residents to stay. Officers involved in the takeover received instruction how to behave.[50] Ramallah radio, controlled by Abdullah, pleaded with the Arabs to stay, saying that the Jews would do no harm.[51] But the frightened villagers did not want to live under Jewish rule, however benevolent. They left, adding to the homeless. Arriving in Amman from Rhodes the three Legion officers who had represented their king were met at the airport by a messenger who warned that public opinion held them responsible for giving up territory, that to avoid being murdered they go quietly home.[52]

Governors of the districts of Samaria and Hebron called on Stabler in mid-April 1949 and said that despite the armistice the Palestinians wanted union with Transjordan.[53] A conference of Palestinian notables had been held at the beginning of December 1948 in Jericho and adopted a resolution that Palestine and Transjordan constituted an indivisible unit; later representatives of municipal councils and refugee groups met in Nablus, called for union, and adopted nine resolutions delivered to the king by two hundred representatives who drove to Amman. It appeared there would be little difficulty with the Palestinians.

But how would the Arab states react to annexation? The Saudi government had expressed concern that if Abdullah took Arab Palestine he would plan for a Greater Syria. Secretary Acheson had assured Jidda that merger of Arab Palestine with Transjordan recommended by the late U.N. mediator had no connection with

Greater Syria.[54] Ibn Saud at the beginning of March sent a message to Abdullah that the fate of the Arabs was bound up with Britain and the United States, that because they had approved annexation he would, but warned against any announcement that might inflame Arab politicians and told the king to go slow.[55]

London wanted Abdullah to proceed quietly. Sir John Troutbeck in the Middle East Office in Cairo said Arab states had an understandable grievance against Abdullah who had been in touch with the Jews at the same time he was proclaiming his desire to throw them into the sea; he told the Jews that he went to war unwillingly, dragged in against his judgment, the sort of thing Laval might have said to Hitler: "Of course one does not expect from the Arabs the same kind of loyalty to each other that one expects but does not always get from Europeans, and it would probably not be difficult to show that many of the Arab leaders are the most perfidious double-crossers."[56] Britain according to Sir Hugh Dow in Jerusalem was indebted to the king because there was no other way out of the Palestine mess.[57]

During Ramadan when in the sweltering countries of the Moslem world the faithful fast from sunrise to sunset, tempers during the daylight hours are short and activity reduced to a minimum. But when King Abdullah visited the Jericho and Ramallah districts of Arab Palestine on July 14, 1949, crowds waited hours to greet him and villages turned out to applaud. Although the king probably had played a part in his reception, British observers reported the people happy.[58]

A month later Abdullah went to London to talk to Bevin.

Apparently the king would not fly with an Arab at the plane's controls. According to Kirkbride, Abdullah explained that he did not want an Arab pilot and said, "I know my own people too well."[59] Through an interpreter Bevin told Abdullah that Palestine was an unfortunate incident. Expressing regret the United States had abandoned the Bernadotte plan he said that at least Washington shared Britain's desire to see Arab Palestine a part of Transjordan. But Bevin refused to set a date. Timing he said, was important.[60]

Abdullah's government began extending its administration into Arab Palestine and Washington and London continued to discuss the issue. The State Department agreed that, yes, Abdullah should have Arab Palestine, but hoped the U.N. could make some arrangement and was reluctant to prepare a timetable for annexation.[61] Once again Washington was unwilling to take responsibility, although it was clear that the U.N. could not solve the Palestine problem. The American government pressed for a U.N. solution. London understood the world organization's limits, and the Foreign Office suggested to Amman that because union would fail without cooperation of the inhabitants, Abdullah should look after Palestinian interests, win the confidence of the population.[62]

The Arab states opposed a union between Transjordan and Arab Palestine, and near the end of 1949 sought to prevent it by fair or foul means. Kirkbride told the Foreign Office the Saudis and Egyptians were planning to set up another government in Palestine, that if they did it Transjordan immediately would

announce incorporation. Speaking about relations among Arab
states a Transjordanian minister said: "There is nothing left
to do but declare war on each other."[63] The Arab League had no
objection to Abdullah's occupation of Arab Palestine but opposed
annexation because Palestine was to be held in trust for its
inhabitants.[64]

Fearing delay would encourage the League, Abdullah with
Kirkbride's blessing decided to announce union, and the Hashemite
Kingdom of Jordan--union of Arab Palestine with Transjordan--was
announced in April 1950. The Palestinian Arabs--those most
concerned--appeared quietly, at least in public, to accept
annexation and the commercial classes were relieved.[65] Here was
victory for the king, and Kirkbride was happy because although
he did not inform London he had decided to resign if instructed
to hold back Abdullah.[66]

The Foreign Office said that the British government intended
to recognize the Kingdom of Jordan, an act designed to increase
Middle Eastern stability, and London wanted Washington to make a
parallel statement. The State Department replied it would be
difficult to announce for union or even find a peg on which to
hang a statement because Washington would have been happier to
postpone annexation. The Department assured the Foreign Office
that the United States was not pressing delay, that the decision
was for Britain.[67] Stabler told Abdullah that although the
United States would not recognize union the fact that relations
with Washington continued without interruption implied
acceptance.[68]

Reaction in Israel was mixed. Tel Aviv told Abdullah that for internal reasons, a vocal minority demanding all of Palestine, Israel could not recognize the union but that the Israeli government hoped the king understood.[69] The British representative in Tel Aviv, Knox Helm, reported that as far as concerned the Israelis the Arab area west of the Jordan River remained a question; although the government accepted union as inevitable Israeli recognition would come with a final settlement.[70]

Announcement of the Kingdom of Jordan did not quiet the Arab League, and it looked as if the League might take action. Secretary General Azzam Pasha said he regretted Abdullah's action and hoped the king would disavow union and describe the relation between his country and Arab Palestine as a trusteeship.[71] At the request of Egypt the Political Committee of the Arab League met at the beginning of May and issued a communique that Jordan had violated League policy, that Lebanon and Egypt recommended expulsion, but that the matter was postponed to allow consultation. The Iraqi government sent a message to Abdullah, uncle of their king, urging him to make a statement to satisfy the League. Kirkbride said Abdullah would not renounce union, so the Foreign Office told the Iraqi government that Britain recognized the Kingdom of Jordan, constitutionally achieved by unanimous vote of the Chamber of Deputies--composed of representatives from both territories--and there was no reason for Abdullah to renounce union. It suggested that at the next League meeting Iraq speak in support of Abdullah.[72] Baghdad

replied that Abdullah was an Arab: if he controlled Arab
Palestine that was better than having the territory fall to the
Jews. Arab leaders knew that eastern Palestine would remain part
of Jordan and were resigned to it, so from his position of
security Abdullah could make the statement demanded by public
opinion, even though meaningless. Getting to the heart of the
matter the Iraqis said if Abdullah refused to give up union the
U.N. could tell the world the Palestine question no longer
existed, that there was no place on the map called Palestine.[73]

Abdullah refused to compromise. The League asked him to
endorse a statement saying the Arab states accepted union until
such time as the whole of Palestine was restored to the Arabs
and then the future of Palestine would be reconsidered. With a
twinkle in his eye Abdullah told Kirkbride that the day the Arab
League conquered Israel he would place all his territory at their
disposal.[74] The League gave up. Reports reached Kirkbride that
the source of the movement to expel Abdullah had been Ibn Saud,
who egged on Farouk, but none of the Arab states wanted to
destroy the League so when the king resisted pressure--something
they had not counted on--they dropped the issue.[75]

In the spring of 1950, two years after establishment of the
Jewish state, it appeared that the Palestine problem had been
resolved; the independent Arab state envisioned in the partition
plan had not emerged, but there were two states in Palestine.
The issue of Arab Palestine thus seemed to have been solved in a
very personal way--the rivalries within Arab states, the ambition
of Abdullah, the preoccupation of the two great Western nations,

Britain and the United States. The succession states of the
Turkish empire despite a generation of tuition by Britain and
France had proved unable to agree on common policy, and there was
in the years after 1945 the increasing ambition of the Saudi
monarch, feeling ever more powerful because of rapidly increasing
oil revenue. Withal the Egyptian monarchy showed itself
incessantly weak, unable to judge any interest, even its own;
the dissolute Farouk sensed none of the internal difficulties of
his regime, and only lived for the moment in Cairo with all of
its elegance and ease. Meanwhile the wily and ambitious Abdullah
knew what he wanted, sensed the importance of Arab territory in
Palestine, and schemed to get it. And the non-Middle Eastern
states, with capitals in London and Washington, looked to other
concerns and rested their diplomacy on chance statements by
Kirkbride, McDonald and Stabler, the British envoy full of
learning and wisdom from long experience in the troubled region,
the Americans full of the new importance of their country,
willing to deal in the currency of Middle Eastern cupidity,
thinking that words would substitute for knowledge, hoping that
whatever happened locally would not affect the great
international interests of their country.

There remained the problem of how to achieve peace. Union
of Arab Palestine with Transjordan did not answer the question of
the Palestinian Arabs and this question received no satisfactory
answer during the years after the Israeli armistice in 1949.
Failure to make peace left a legacy of feeling that plagued both
Arabs and Jews, a legacy that neither side could afford.

The personalities in the situation were of course obviously
opposed, although one might have expected a better result because
both David Ben-Gurion and King Abdullah were subtle men,
accustomed to the need for compromise in all aspects of life,
ready to see beyond exigencies of the moment. Ben-Gurion had
spent his life working for a Jewish state and in his sixty-second
year the stocky white-haired Zionist leader born in Poland had
proclaimed the State of Israel. Settling in Palestine in 1906,
the future prime minister worked in the orange groves and
vineyards. His leadership was quickly recognized and in 1911 he
was elected a delegate to the eleventh Zionist Congress, held in
Vienna. Afterward he studied law in Salonika and Constantinople,
to prepare to deal with the Turkish rulers of Palestine, but when
during the First World War the British government announced the
Balfour Declaration, Ben-Gurion called for a Jewish battalion to
liberate Palestine and volunteered for the British army. He
continued with the British until London withdrew support for a
Jewish national home, and then led the struggle to get the

British out of Palestine. He had a prophetic vision of
ingathering of the exiles--return of the remnant of the children
of Israel to their homeland. But he was essentially a modern
nationalist who wanted to build a socialist, democratic state, to
provide fulfillment and security. Without peace such a state was
impossible.

As for Abdullah, he too had come up in life through arduous
effort. On behalf of his father, thirty-seventh in line of
descent from the Prophet Mohammed, Grand Sherif of Mecca,
Abdullah Ibn Hussein in 1914 had called on High Commissioner Lord
Kitchener in Cairo. The Hashemites were unhappy with Turkish
rule, and desired to lead an Arab revolt. When Turkey joined the
Central Powers the British worked out an arrangement with Hussein
and his sons, and as a result the Arabs fought with the British.
After victory Abdullah was to have the throne of Iraq, but
matters did not work out as planned when the French drove his
brother Feisal from Syria and it appeared that the British wanted
to give Iraq to Feisal as an exchange for the throne he had lost.
With a small group of followers the ambitious Abdullah instead
entered Transjordan, and the British agreed that he could stay.
Later Ibn Saud marshalled the extremist, puritanical Wahabis, who
lived according to the strict rules of the Koran, and drove
Hussein out of the Hejaz. Abdullah in dusty Amman, virtually a
British satrap, dreamed of leading a new Arab revolt that would
unite the Arabs under his rule. Reviewing troops in May 1949, on
Jordan's Army Day, which celebrated his accession to the throne
three years before, the king told the Legion he intended to

continue towards a united Arab Kingdom as envisaged by his father Hussein, and compared his soldiers to "the holy Arab Army" that unified the Arab world at the time of Mohammad. Abdullah was an Arab nationalist, but unlike Ben-Gurion he wanted to expand so as to rule an empire, an empire that he could pass on to a new generation of Hashemites.

Abdullah and Ben-Gurion had different goals, but both wanted peace. Ben-Gurion considered Abdullah the Arab head-of-state most likely to cooperate with Israel and at the worst of times had tried to maintain communication. When Jewish terrorists in April 1948 attacked an Arab village on the outskirts of Jerusalem, Dir Yassin, leaving more than 200 dead, including women and children, Ben-Gurion approved a Jewish Agency telegram to Abdullah expressing shock and regret.[1]

Israel assuredly needed peace; the new state had opened its doors to the European DP's, beginning the ingathering of the exiles, not only Europeans but Jews from Arab countries came to Israel. Housing was scarce, and a large proportion of immigrants lived in camps, receiving meals from central kitchens. Massive immigration aggravated economic difficulties; taxation rose as productivity declined. There were shortages of almost everything, necessitating rationing of food and clothing. Peace would allow Israel to concentrate on social and economic problems.

Jordan likewise needed peace; the king wanted to strengthen his enlarged kingdom whose population, mostly of Bedouin descent, was now overwhelmed by newcomers. Jordan like Israel suffered from a shortage of housing; refugees in camps depended on charity. Peace would permit economic development, and allow Abdullah to move forward with his dreams of a Greater Syria.

Britain in the spring of 1950 did not yet desire Jordan to make peace with Israel. The British government despite objection from the Arab League finally agreed to Abdullah's annexation of Arab Palestine, but when it came to the question of peace-making London continued to tell Abdullah that he had to consider the Arab states. The British government accepted the Jewish state, granted de facto recognition, but doubted Jewish good intentions--a gentlemanly sort of anti-Semitism. Even before the first Representative to Israel, Sir Alexander Knox Helm, arrived in Tel Aviv, Helm said the Israeli government had offered quarters in two dimly-lit basement rooms and done nothing about residences for himself and his staff. The Israelis also protested a member of his staff before the appointment was announced. According to Helm, Britain could not let Israel get away with such behavior because "it would merely mean that the Israelis would feel that they could kick us around as they like and that we ourselves should be thoroughly demeaned in the process."[2] The Foreign Office saw Israel as a danger to British interests, and hoped for the collapse of the Jewish state ("If it does tant mieux so long as we have retained Arab friendship in the interval.")[3]

How to establish relations with Israel friendly enough to please the United States, and at the same time prevent antagonizing the Arabs? Sir Oliver Franks who the previous spring replaced Inverchapel in Washington reported a letter from Israeli Ambassador Eliahu Elath; London told Franks to keep social relations at the minimum consistent with courtesy, that he should not cut the Israeli ambassador at diplomatic receptions, nor should he go out of his way to invite him to dinner.[4]

Helm arrived in Israel and reported his reception cordial, no indication of hostility except faded signs on walls in Hebrew and English, "British invaders out of our country." The American ambassador was suppose to be the most popular foreigner but Israelis considered McDonald's popularity more apparent than real, and among respondible people he was a "laughing stock."[5] Writing to Bevin, Helm said the Israelis wanted friendly relations, that the foreign secretary was not their hero, that Jews remained suspicious of Britain's motives, "not lessened by the intense inferiority complex from which so many Jews suffer." Helm said he tried reassuring the Israelis that if Britain's purpose was so nefarious he would not be in Tel Aviv.[6]

Visiting Helm, Foreign Minister Sharett asked if the British government accepted Israel or if London was still hoping for collapse of the Jewish state. The Foreign Office instructed Helm to say the British attitude would be determined by the Israeli attitude, that Israel had to accept Britain as a great power with important interests in the Middle East--preservation of Western civilization.[7] The Foreign Office considered de jure recognition and decided the best time would be after the British government recognized Abdullah's annexation of Arab Palestine.[8]

After several months in Israel, Helm gained respect for the

Israelis and wanted the Foreign Office to take a new look. Returning from a visit to Cairo in April 1950 he reported Egypt depressing, the Arab world headed for chaos. Since withdrawal of Britain's leadership, Arab countries had lost direction. The British government might one day need to look to the Israelis and he pleaded that London encourage Abdullah to make peace.[9]

After the armistice in April 1949 the Foreign Office told Abdullah to rely on the U.N. for a settlement with Israel. But when two months after armistice talks no progress was being made at the U.N.-sponsored Lausanne Conference, Abdullah agreed to Israel's request to negotiate a bilateral agreement.[10] The king pressed for a port, and the Israelis appeared unwilling to help.

Jordan's minister in Washington, Yusuf Haikal, visited the State Department to explain his country needed a band of territory giving access to the sea and protested that Israel had offered a narrow corridor. The Assistant Secretary of State for Near Eastern Affairs, George C. McGhee, said he doubted feasibility of any corridor, that Jordan could obtain the same advantage by means of a free port, but final decision was up to Jordan. Haikal asked if the Department had any message for the king, and McGhee said that the United States appreciated Jordan's willingness to talk with Israel and hoped talks would continue.[11]

Washington wanted settlement but was unwilling to get mixed up in details, so Ambassador Franks reported at the end of January 1950; the State Department said there was no need for Abdullah to seek concession from Israel with which to justify himself to the Arab states, that the king could ignore Arab opinion, look after his country's interests, reach a settlement on the line of present boundaries with minor modification.[12] The Department was hopeful Israel and Jordan would work together to reach settlement.

The Israeli expert on Arab affairs who had led his country's delegation to the Rhodes armistice talks, Reuven Shiloah, wrote Jordan's Minister of Foreign Affairs, Samir Pasha, in February 1950 proposing a private meeting of himself, Samir, and Abdullah. A month before, Samir had requested that he go to Israel to discuss the corridor problem with Ben-Gurion, and the Israelis sent word that the prime minister would welcome Samir, but no progress was possible until Amman modified its position. Although anxious for settlement, Abdullah agreed that it would be a mistake to appear to be running after the Israelis.[13] Now the Jordanians agreed to receive Shiloah. Dayan accompanied Shiloah, and at first it appeared they would have to give up without agreement. Talk was not going to achieve a solution unless there was compromise.

Abdullah wanted action, and to Shiloah he dictated new proposals: a five-year nonaggression pact with present armistice lines, appointment of technical committees to consider adjustment of armistice lines into a frontier, compensation by Israel for Arab property in the New City of Jerusalem, permission for refugees with property in Israel to return to liquidate the property, a free zone in Haifa with harbor and transit rights, access for Israelis to the Hebrew University on Mount Scopus. Dayan and Shiloah were happy with the proposals, and Shiloah said

there was a possibility for progress.[14] Both sides agreed to
prepare detailed drafts of the agreement. The agreement was not
to become a treaty but supplement to the armistice protocols.[15]

But once more Kirkbride warned Abdullah of Jewish
intentions, the danger that Israel accept some proposals and
amend others. Kirkbride asked how the public would react to a
nonaggression pact and what would happen if Arabs returning to
Israel had to liquidate property under unfair terms. Abdullah
did not want to lose a settlement and told Kirkbride he was not
worried about public opinion, that even if Arab property in
Israel was liquidated unfairly it would be an improvement over
not getting anything.[16]

Abdullah's hopes were dashed when he put forward the
settlement--terms he had proposed--to his government. The prime
minister resigned, returning to office only after the king agreed
to postpone action until after elections scheduled for April
1950, elections both in Transjordan and Arab Palestine.[17] The
king wanted Anglo-American help but did not get it. The British
government refused to intervene, explaining that it would play
into the hands of xenophobic elements, and that for the American
government to intervene would be less advisable because the Arab
League would say the United States had aided the Jews by dividing
the Arabs.[18]

The Ben-Gurion government was unwilling to give up. Israel
asked both the United States and Britain to press for a
settlement, to speak for peace. Ambassador Helm told the Foreign
Office he was confused, that he thought London favored

negotiation between Abdullah and Israel, that London wanted a settlement.[19] The Foreign Office explained that Britain wanted peace but not at any price, that the Israelis had received more than their share of Palestine, that any settlement should involve more territory. Admitting Israel might never be willing to make territorial concessions, that Transjordan might have to agree to an unfair settlement, the Foreign Office said that regardless of what Abdullah wanted London would not ask the king's government to accept an unfair arrangement, and that since by the middle of April a new Jordanian assembly would be in office and Arab Palestine incorporated in Jordan, it appeared wise to wait.[20]

The pour parleurs continued, to not much avail. Foreign Minister Sharett visited Ambassador McDonald at the beginning of March to plead that the United States encourage Abdullah to continue talks, that Washington give the king secret assurance of moral and economic support. According to Sharett, Abdullah was willing to break with the Arab boycott, to trade with Israel, so Egypt and Iraq might cut off rice and sugar to Amman. Hence Jordan needed assurance that Washington would help. The Foreign Minister suggested a personal message from President Truman to King Abdullah.[21]

The American ambassador, McDonald, wanted to help. The president had appointed him to Tel Aviv without consulting Secretary Marshall and the State Department did not approve, so when McDonald had a matter of urgency he appealed directly to Truman. Now he cabled the president that the Israeli-Jordanian nonaggression pact could be saved if he would send a personal

message to Abdullah. President Truman discussed the cable with
Acheson who said the king's difficulties were with members of his
own government, that Abdullah had agreed not to press for the
Treaty until after elections. According to Acheson a
presidential message would leak and the king might find himself
the principal issue in those elections. Truman decided against
a message.[22]

Meanwhile Ambassador Helm told London that McDonald
conducted most of his activities from his house, that he rarely
went to the chancery, that he was too close to the Israelis so it
was impossible to speak freely with him.[23] McDonald in August
traveled to the United States and Helm was disappointed he did
not stay there. After his return Helm, walking his dog, met the
ambassador who was on his way to his commercial secretary's
house. Helm told the Foreign Office that the commercial
secretary was a Jew, that it was doubtful if foreign Jews in
Israel could be loyal to their own country. Later McDonald
bragged that when he was in New York he succeeded in getting his
grandson to call him sava and his wife savta--Hebrew for
grandfather and grandmother. According to Helm this was one more
reason to suspect McDonald.[24]

After establishment of the Kingdom of Jordan, Israel once
more tried for an agreement. Taking into account Kirkbride's
role in Jordanian affairs, Shiloah asked to meet both the king
and the ambassador. Helm told the Foreign Office that while
Kirkbride had been keeping his American colleague in Amman
informed about his views and instructions, information had been

reported to Washington and then passed to Tel Aviv--that was a problem because McDonald told the Israelis everything.[25] Kirkbride refused to talk to any Israeli representative; he told Abdullah not to do anything that might bring him into conflict with his new parliament.[26]

Israel celebrated its second independence day according to the lunar calendar on April 23, 1950, with festivities in the new city of Jerusalem; crowds danced all night in flood-lit streets, and more than 100,000 people watched a military parade that passed near Arab Legion outposts on the walls of the old city. Foreign diplomats were conspicuously absent from the reviewing stand because the U.N. had called for internationalization of Jerusalem--holy to Christians, Moslems and Jews. Both Israel and Jordan opposed internationalization and had in effect partitioned Jerusalem between them. After Israel's first election the Ben-Gurion government had announced that the Parliament, known as Knesset, would meet in Jerusalem. McDonald asked for State Department permission to attend opening ceremonies, but the Department told him to stay in Tel Aviv, that Jerusalem was not part of Israel. Now the American ambassador unable to participate in Jerusalem joined his colleagues at a party given by Tel Aviv's Mayor Israel Rokach.[27]

Legion troops sitting on the stone walls of the old city watched the Israeli independence day parade through binoculars. A Zionist reporter at the parade commented that diplomatic circles hinted rapprochement between Israel and Jordan and perhaps next year Abdullah's troops would view the parade from the grandstand as guests of the Israeli government. There was still hope for peace.[28]

During the summer of 1950 frontier incidents on the Israeli-Jordanian border increased; Arabs crossed into Israel to visit relatives or return to their lands; Arabs--a minority--crossed into Israel to steal, rape, and murder. The Israeli government's concern was lives and property. Forces patrolling the border did not distinguish between innocent and criminal intentions; Tel Aviv's policy appeared to be shoot first. Innocent people died or were injured.

Union stiffened the Jordanian government's resistance to settlement. Palestinian Arabs did not want peace. The Jordanian minister in Cairo explained that his country had been searching for security, that because Britain had recognized annexation of Arab Palestine and extended the Anglo-Jordanian Treaty to cover the territory a settlement with Israel was no longer needed. The only country willing to make peace with Israel drew back.[28]

Perhaps if the American government had taken a role peace would still have been possible, but 1950 was a difficult year for the Truman administration, and the Middle East was not a high priority area. Some Americans, upset by the fall of China to the Communists, blamed the State Department for Russia's growing power, and suspicion remained even after Acheson in August 1949 released a White Paper that presented facts--the United States could not have prevented establishment of the People's Republic of China. Fear of communism produced panic, and a vocal group of Americans described as primitives by Acheson, suspected there

were many traitors in the United States, traitors working for the
Soviet Union. Ironically, the tall aristocratic ivy league-
educated secretary of state, an outspoken Cold Warrior, became a
target of the primitives. The unsavory Senator Joseph R.
McCarthy spoke to a group of Republican women in Wheeling, West
Virginia, in February 1950 claiming that the State Department was
infested with communists. Thus began what was to become a witch
hunt, destroying reputations and careers. Acheson and the
president had to stand up to attack and even to a Republican-
sponsored request for the secretary's removal.

Acheson went to Europe in May 1950 to attend a ministerial
meeting of the North Atlantic Treaty Council, and before boarding
the presidential plane Independence called on free men and free
nations to summon their moral and material strength for vigorous
action against communism.[30] After a short visit to Paris,
Acheson arrived in London on May 9 the day announcement was made
that West German Chancellor Konrad Adenauer had accepted an
invitation for his country to join the Council of Europe as an
associate member, and that the United States would aid France in
resisting communist rebellion in Indo-China.[31] Acheson held
tripartite meetings with Bevin and French Foreign Minister Robert
Schuman; the focus of these meetings was how best to meet the
Soviet menace, but attention was given to the Middle East.
Acheson has opposed a Jewish state and now wanted an even-handed
policy toward Arabs and Jews so he suggested a declaration saying
that the three powers--Britain, France, and the United States--
would supply arms to the Arab states and Israel on a balanced

basis, but only to those governments that promised not to commit aggression. Bevin and Schuman agreed and the Tripartite Declaration was announced.

Western attention turned to the Far East when on June 25, 1950, North Korean troops crossed the 38th parallel into South Korea in an action seen as another attempt by the Soviet Union to challenge the West. Secretary Acheson called an emergency meeting of the U.N. Security Council, and when North Korea ignored a Council request to withdraw--made possible because the Soviet Union was boycotting the U.N. over refusal to seat Communist China--the Council condemned North Korea as an aggressor and called on member states to aid the Republic of Korea. The United States went to war under the U.N., and the British government supported the Americans.

Aggression in Korea underlined the importance of the Middle East. But there was no set program for bringing peace. No help from Britain or the United States was available; Israel and Jordan were on their own to work things out as best they could.

Abdullah wanted peace, and yet his ministers who after union had more authority held back. The king explained that there could be no development, no economic improvement, no security without peace, that Jordanians wanted peace. One of the nine Nablus Resolutions presented to the king at the end of 1949 had called for hostilities with Israel; Abdullah ignored it. Once more Jordan's ministers heard that people opposed peace, any sort of settlement with Israel. The Palestinian Arabs who were Abdullah's subjects still wanted to drive the Jews into the sea to regain all Palestine. When these findings were reported to the king he was angry and decided to dismiss his ministers. Kirkbride said the king was obsessed with recovering his fatherland from Ibn Saud, that he insisted on settlement with Israel because this was the first step in taking Mecca, in creating the Hashemite Kingdom of Greater Syria. According to Kirkbride, Abdullah did not care about the terms of settlement with Israel; he wanted any settlement the Jews were willing to approve.[32]

The Ben-Gurion government did not give up, and continued efforts to negotiate. The Israeli ambassador called on the Foreign Office in the middle of September to say that peace was urgent in view of the international situation, communist aggression in Korea. He said the Soviet Minister in Syria was working to obstruct negotiation, that the British, who had considerable influence, should press the Jordanians, that it was unfortunate Abdullah, who had been so close to peace, was no longer able to arrange it, but the key lay in Britain's hands. Britain could unlock the door by assuring Amman that in event of trouble with the Arab League the British would assist the Jordanians.[33] No mention of what Britain could do if the Arab Palestinians, now Abdullah's subjects, caused trouble.

Replacing Elath as ambassador to the United States in September 1950, Abba Eban presented his credentials to President Truman. Eban arrived at the White House dressed in black homburg, morning suit, and gray tie and entered the Oval Office where Truman was seated behind his desk with his jacket off, bright red suspenders visible. The president rose to greet the new ambassador, took the credentials and prepared speech from him, and said "Let's cut out all the crap and have a good talk." The president and Eban talked for forty minutes.[34] But talk did not help bring peace.

Abdullah could not find ministers willing to settle with Israel. Israeli agents visited the king in the beginning of October 1950, and Abdullah told Kirkbride the Ben-Gurion government had requested the meeting, but the British ambassador had seen a message from Tel Aviv claiming the king had invited the Israelis to Amman. Abdullah wanted to order his ministers to make contact with the Israeli government, and despite opposition from Kirkbride gave an order. Once more his ministers resigned. After ten days of threatening, promising, coaxing, he was unable to put together a cabinet willing to negotiate. The king sent word to Tel Aviv that he had failed.

The Israeli government held the British responsible and accused Kirkbride, maintaining that Kirkbride would not go farther than he felt justified, that he had the confidence of his government, that he was in position to make the decision.[36] Helm visited Jordan in November; the ambassador attended several social functions and during conversation heard anti-Semitic remarks from both the Arab and British communities. Kirkbride told him renewal of negotiations was unlikely, that it was best to allow for time.[37]

A disappointed Shiloah saw Abdullah in December and the king addressed him with the term of endearment *azziz*, but there was no way to break the deadlock. Shiloah said Israel was ready to compromise, that Israel wanted peace, and Abdullah asked his former defense minister now Prime Minister, Samir, at least to meet the Israelis. Samir refused, saying enemies accused him of taking office to come to terms with the Jews, that he often had heard of Israeli goodwill but never saw evidence of it.[38]

Efforts to make peace had failed. The Arab League continued to plot destruction of Israel. Arab leaders overwhelmed by problems at home, growing discontent with rulers considered greedy, selfish, lackeys of the West, promoted anti-Israel sentiment, and regularly announced intention to renew war. Meanwhile forces were gathering that would remove some of the old leaders from power replacing them with militant nationalists who would turn away from the West, exploit the Palestinians, and refuse negotiation.

Washington and London at the end of 1950 were absorbed with the Korean conflict and the fear that the Soviets might move in Europe. Acheson had decided it was essential to defend the West as far east as possible, that German troops had to be included in NATO. The Americans and British tried to convince the reluctant French to accept German participation and were successful when Truman announced more American soldiers to Europe and appointment of General Dwight D. Eisenhower as commander of NATO forces. At a press conference in the middle of December, President Truman spoke out in defense of Acheson who was still under attack: "If communism were to prevail in the world--as it shall not prevail-- Dean Acheson would be one of the first, if not the first, to be shot by the enemies of liberty and Christianity."[39] There were

so many problems demanding attention that Israel and Jordan, the

Jews and the Arabs had to get along the best they could without

Anglo-American participation.

Anglo-American effort to find a solution to Palestine had

failed, and years of unrest punctuated by war and terrorist

activity followed. The Soviets used every opportunity to take

advantage of the situation, and until the visit of Egyptian

President Anwar el-Sadat to Jerusalem in November 1977 no Arab

leader except Abdullah, assassinated in 1951, dared proclaim a

desire to recognize the Jewish state, to live in peace with

Israel.

British and Americans were unsuccessful not out of lack of

understanding or indifference. There were too many conflicting

interests.

The Jews, burdened by a terrible history that equated their

almost two-thousand-year exile with insecurity, degradation, and

fear, were in the initial stages of trying to comprehend what had

happened to their people in Europe. Enraged by the slaughter,

the Jewish community in Palestine, morally and financially

supported by American Jewry, determined to establish a state.

They had no sympathy for the Palestinian Arabs. Since there were

so many Arab countries the Jews wanted to know why the Arab world

did not care for Arab refugees in the same way world Jewry cared

for Jewish refugees.

During the last years of the mandate the Zionists had no

confidence in the British government. When the British

championed proposals, the Anglo-American Committee of Inquiry, the Cabinet Committee, London Conference, Bernadotte plan, Jews saw attempts to prevent a Jewish state and claimed the British were looking after their own interests and not trying to find a solution. As for Zionists the British government in 1917 had promised to protect the Jews, to support a Jewish national home in Palestine; promises had not been kept, the Jews betrayed in their darkest hour.

Zionists looked to the American government. Since the United States had the largest remaining Jewish community the Jewish Agency and Israeli government expected and received support. Between 1945 and 1950 it often appeared that Zionists wanted to drive a wedge between London and Washington to prevent Anglo-American efforts to reach a solution contrary to Zionist goals.

The Arab states looked to Britain. After the Second World War they wanted to expel European powers and achieve the self-determination promised in 1914-1918. Although the Arabs wanted the British out, most Arab leaders in power depended on European advice and European finance. Zionists were intruders who took land that belonged to Arabs. After the Second World War the Arabs expected British help because the British government had issued the Balfour Declaration. If the British wanted Arab friendship they had to prevent a Jewish state, undo the damage of the Balfour Declaration. When it was clear that nothing could prevent establishment of Israel, the Arabs wanted British support to keep Israel isolated, to prevent peace.

Beset by economic problems the postwar Labor government was unable to handle the Palestine issue. London asked Washington for help, but the Attlee government resented Americans, the fact that British weakness necessitated calling on the United States. The Palestine problem was complicated by Anglo-American rivalry; Foreign Office officials had been educated to take up the white man's burden, rule empire, and now saw the dominance of the United States. The British were grateful for the American loan and later for the Marshall plan, but American generosity underlined dependence. The Foreign Office was sensitive. Because of Britain's experience in the Middle East, London had expected to put forward policies that Washington would accept and carry out.

When the American government refused the solution Britain wanted--a solution acceptable to the Arabs--the British blamed the Jews. It was not that the British denied that Jews had suffered during the war: the British did not understand the need of Palestine. Regretting the Balfour Declaration, the British government was interested in keeping the Soviet Union out of the Middle East. It appeared to London that the political importance of American Jewry interfered with plans, that President Truman was willing to sacrifice Anglo-American interests for the Jewish vote. Then there were personalities. Foreign Secretary Bevin was outspoken, too brash to handle this problem, and exacerbated the situation. Moreover the British presence in the Middle East caused political problems at home; British lives were lost.

The United States was in the best position to do something,

to solve the Palestine problem. Although the American government in 1950 sent troops to Korea, the Truman administration was never willing to send troops to Palestine. Washington considered Korea a clear-cut case of Soviet aggression. But the situation in Palestine was different; it seemed that if the United States were to send troops the Truman administration would be inviting a Soviet response, and so after the U.N. voted partition the American government refused to carry it out. Hence before establishment of the Jewish state an opportunity to impose a U.N. settlement was lost. The Truman administration had agreed to work with Britain, but Washington did not want to take over for the British, to assume responsibilities in Palestine. Although most State Department officials shared the opinion of the British in regard to keeping Arab friendship they resented criticism of policy, and objected to what they considered Britain's evasion of responsibility. Washington was willing to help, to offer assistance, but not to replace. The American government refused to go further than participate in the Anglo-American Committee of Inquiry, the Cabinet Committee, and offer moral support to the U.N.-sponsored partition.

After establishment of Israel it seemed to London that the Jews were happy. The Truman administration considered the problem solved. The Attlee government explained the importance of arranging for union of Transjordan and Arab Palestine. Once Abdullah had his Kingdom of Jordan there were Anglo-American conversations about a final settlement between Arabs and Jews, but the conversations did not lead to anything. Settlement was left to the U.N.; Abdullah was not given support to achieve a breakthrough.

Neither the British nor the Americans understood that solving what was called the Jewish problem had created an Arab problem, that the displaced Palestinians would not be satisfied with Jordanian rule or resettlement, that while it appeared that the Palestinians had no leaders--at least no respectable leaders--these Arabs would not forget their homeland, would refuse to allow either the Jews or the rest of the world to live in peace. Anglo-American failure left a legacy. Palestine did not disappear from the map. The Palestinians became symbols, to some observers despicable terrorists, to others freedom fighters, but to all a serious unresolved international concern.

NOTES FOR CHAPTER 1

[1]David W. Levy and Melvin I. Urofsky (ed.), Letters of Louis
D. Brandeis Vol. IV (Albany: State Univ. of N.Y., 1975), p. 288.

[2]Cyrus Adler, Jacob H. Schiff: His Life And Letters Vol. II
(Garden City: Doubleday, 1929), p. 307.

[3]Irwin Oder, "The United States and the Palestine Mandate,
1920-1948; A Study of the Impact of Interest Groups on Foreign
Policy" (Ph.D. dissertation, Columbia Univ., 1956), p. 22.

[4]David Lloyd George, War Memoirs Vol. IV (Boston: Little
Brown, 1934), p. 75.

[5]Hadassah Newsletter, May 1921, p. 1.

[6]Lawrence Evans, United States Policy And The Partition Of
Turkey, 1914-1924 (Baltimore: John Hopkins, 1965), p. 135.

[7]Phillip J. Baram, The Department Of State In The Middle
East, 1919-1945 (Philadelphia: Univ. of Pennsylvania, 1978),
p. 247.

[8]John Bowle, Viscount Samuel (London: Gollancz, 1957),
p. 23.

[9]Hadassah Newsletter, March 1921, p. 1.

[10]New Palestine, September 6, 1929, pp. 149-150.

[11]Baram, p. 249.

[12]New Palestine, September 6, 1929, p. 141.

[13]Ibid., June 5, 1936, p. 1.

[14]Ibid., November 13, 1936, p. 1.

[15]Ibid., November 27, 1936, p. 1.

[16]Ibid., January 22, 1937, pp. 1-2.

[17]Michael J. Cohen, Palestine: Retreat From The Mandate (New York: Holmes & Meier, 1978), p. 35.

[18]New Palestine, April 29, 1938, p. 3.

[19]Baram, p. 252.

[20]Ibid., p. 255.

[21]Loy W. Henderson, Oral History, Harry S. Truman Library, Independence, Missouri (hereafter called HSTL).

[22]Arthur D. Morse, While Six Million Died (New York: Random House, 1968), p. 29.

[23]Bernard Wasserstein, Britain And The Jews Of Europe 1939-1945 (London: Clarendon, 1979), p. 50.

[24]Francis L. Loewenheim, Harold D. Langley, Manfred Jonas (ed.), Roosevelt And Churchill: Their Secret Wartime Correspondence (New York: Dutton, 1975), p. 73.

[25]Wasserstein, p. 348.

[26]Loewenheim, Langley, Jonas, pp. 566-567.

[27]Anthony R. Deluca, "Der Gross Mufti in Berlin," International Journal of Middle East Studies, February 1979, pp. 125-138.

[1]Great Britain, Parliament, Hansard's Parliamentary Debates (Commons), 5th Series, 410 (1945): (hereafter cited as Hansard), p. 1904.

[2]New Palestine, April 30, 1945, p. 1.

[3]Chaim Weizmann, Trial And Error (New York: Schocken, 1949), p. 456.

[4]Hansard, 415 (1945): 608.

[5]Francis Williams, A Prime Minister Remembers; The War And PostWar Memoirs Of Earl Attlee (London: Heinemann, 1961), p. 189.

[6]The Prime Minister to the President, London, September 14, 1945, Lot 56 D359, Diplomatic Records of the Department of State, National Archives, Washington, DC (hereafter cited as NA).

[7]The Diary of Eben A. Ayers, September 19, 1945, p. 159, HSTL.

[8]Hansard, 415 (1945): 1925.

[9]Time, November 19, 1945, p. 36.

[10]Ibid., January 28, 1946.

[11]Letter, Byrnes to the Embassy in London, Washington, December 3, 1945, 841.111 11/1-445, NA.

[12]Great Britain, Cabinet (hereafter cited as Cab.), 128/5, Cabinet Minutes (hereafter cited as CM), 1946, 38, April 29, 1946, p. 302. Public Records Office, Kew, England (hereafter cited as PRO).

[13]Cab. 128/6 CM (46) 91. October 25, 1946, p. 93, PRO.

[14]Telegram 1981, Bevin to the Foreign Office, New York, November 26, 1946, FO 371/52565 (E 1610/4131), PRO.

[15]The United States DP Commission, Memo To America: The DP Story (Washington: USGPO, 1952), p. 9.

[16]Ibid., p. 15.

[17]Hansard, 433 (1947): 1919.

[18]Telegram 5840, Bevin to Inverchapel, London, June 14, 1946, FO 371/52529 (E 544/4131), PRO.

[19]Memorandum, Mason to Dixon, London, June 18, 1946, FO 371/52520 (E 5700/4/31), PRO.

[20]Williams, p. 134.

[21]C. Hartley Grattan, "Notes On Britain Today," Harper's, June 1946, p. 570.

[22]Cab. 128/6 CM (46) 66, July 8, 1946, p. 181, PRO.

[23]Times (London), July 5, 1946, p. 4.

[24]Telegram 35, Foreign Office to Inverchapel, London, January 1, 1947, FO 371/61799 (E 73/48/31), PRO.

[25]Telegram 216, Bevin to the Foreign Office, Moscow, March 20, 1947, FO 371/6161770 (E 2415/46/31), PRO.

[26]Embassy to the Secretary of State, London, August 3, 1947, 867N.01/8-347, NA; Memorandum of a Conversation between the American Ambassador and the Foreign Secretary, London, August 4, 1947, FO 371/61821 (E 7167/48/31), PRO.

[27]The Secretary of State to the Attorney General, Washington, August 7, 1947, 867N.01/8-747, NA.

[28]Telegram 4471, Balfour to the Foreign Office, Washington, August 14, 1947, FO 371/61822 (E 7490/48/31), PRO.

[29]Telegram 3666, Lovett to the Embassy in London, Washington, August 25, 1947, 867N.01/8-2247, NA.

[30]Note by J. G. S. Beith, London, August 29, 1947, FO 371/ 61824 (E 7938/48/31), PRO.

[31]The New York Times, September 11, 1947, p. 52; Ibid., September 14, 1947, p. 52.

[32]Ruth Gruber, Destination Palestine (U.S.A.: Statford, 1948), pp. 51-52.

[33]Christopher Sykes, Crossroads To Israel, 1914-1948 (Bloomington: Indiana University, 1973), p. 323; John Marlowe, The Seat Of Pilate (London: Cresset, 1959), p. 232.

[34]Hansard, 426 (1946): 130.

[35]The Attorney General to the Secretary of State, Washington, September 24, 1947, 867N.01/9-447, NA.

[36]Memorandum of a Conversation between the General Counsel Customs Division, Treasury Department, Office of the Assistant Secretary of the Treasury, and the Legal Division, Department of State, Washington, November 17, 1947, 867N.01/11-1747, NA.

[37]The Secretary of State to the British Foreign Secretary, Washington, November 7, 1947, Foreign Relations of the United States 1947, Vol. V (Washington: GPO, 1953) (hereafter cited as FRUS), pp. 1247-1248; Memorandum of a Conversation between the Legal Division of the State Department and the Admiralty Division of the Justice Department, Washington, November 12, 1947, 867N.01/11-1047, NA.

[38]Telegram 6923, Inverchapel to the Foreign Office, FO 371/ 61859 (E 11724/95/31), PRO.

[39]Memorandum of a Conversation between the Legal Division of the State Department and Derecktor, Washington, November 21, 1947, 867N.01/11-1747, NA.

[40]Minutes of a Meeting on Illegal Immigration, London, October 15, 1947, FO 371/61850 (E 9830/84/31), PRO.

[41]Memorandum of a Conversation, Washington, January 21, 1948, 867N.01/1-2148, NA.

[42]Picture in the Collection of Samuel Derecktor, Scarsdale, New York.

[1]Memorandum, Rosenman to Truman, Washington, October 23, 1945, Papers of Samuel I. Rosenman, HSTL.

[2]Transcript of a Conversation between Halifax and Byrnes, Washington, October 22, 1945, Lot 56D 359, NA.

[3]Memorandum, Byrnes to Truman, Washington, October 30, 1945, President's Secretary's File (hereafter cited as PSF), Foreign Affairs, HSTL.

[4]Williams, p. 193.

[5]Hansard, 415 (1945): 1927.

[6]The New York Times, November 14, 1945, p. 12.

[7]Telegram 7717, Halifax to the Foreign Office, Washington, November 17, 1945, FO 371/45402 (E 8861/265/31), PRO; Telegram 1194, Embassy to Byrnes, London, November 14, 1945, 867N.01/11/1445, NA.

[8]Minute by Morgan, London, undated, FO 371/52504 (E 2621/4/31), PRO.

[9]Letter, Byrnes to Halifax, Washington, November 25, 1945, 867N.01/11-2524, NA.

[10]Telegram 7959, Halifax to the Foreign Office, Washington, undated, FO 371/45387 (E 9269/15/31), PRO.

[11]Henderson Oral History, pp. 108-110, HSTL.

[12]Bartley C. Crum, Behind The Silken Curtain (New York: Simon & Schuster, 1947), p. 5.

[13]Richard Crossman, Palestine Mission (New York: Harper, 1947), pp. 10-16.

[14]Telegram 12776, FO to Halifax, London, December 20, 1945, FO 371/45389 (E 9828/15/31), PRO.

[15]Crossman, p. 14.

[16]Telegram 8447, Halifax to the Foreign Office, Washington, December 19, 1945, FO 371/45389 (E 9969/15/31), PRO.

[17]Telegram 616, Ibid., December 10, 1945, FO 371/44539 (An 3788/4/45), PRO.

[18]Memorandum, January 11, 1946, Papers of James G. McDonald, Herbert H. Lehman Papers (hereafter cited as HHL), Columbia University, New York City.

[19]Ibid., January 23, 1946, Ibid.

[20]Crossman, p. 52.

[21]Memorandum, February 1, 1946, Papers of James G. McDonald, HHL.

[22]Crossman, p. 79.

[23]Papers of James G. McDonald, February 13, 1946, HHL.

[24]Telegram 1124, Halifax to the Foreign Office, Washington, February 19, 1946, FO 371/52510 (E 1518/4/31), PRO.

[25]Papers of James G. McDonald, March 1, 1946, HHL.

[26]Ibid., April 3, 1946, Ibid.

[27]Ibid., April 20, 1946, Ibid.

[28]Bevin to Foreign Office, Paris, April 27, 1945, FO 371/ 52517 (E 3786/4/31), PRO.

[29]Cab. 128/5 CM (46) 38, April 29, 1946, p. 301, PRO.

[30]Francis Williams, Ernest Bevin, Portrait Of A Great Englishman (London: Hutchinson, 1952), p. 260.

[31]Memorandum, Acheson to Henderson, Washington, May 6, 1946,

867N.01/5-646, NA.

[32]Cab. 128/5 CM (46) 50, May 20, 1946, p. 7, PRO.

[33]Lord Boothby, My Yesterday Your Tomorrow (London:
Hutchinson, 1962), p. 69.

[34]Telegram 159, Grafftey Smith to the Foreign Office, Jidda,
April 23, 1946, FO 371/52516 (E 3663/4/31), PRO.

[35]Telegram 87, Lord Killearn to the Foreign Office, Cairo,
January 17, 1946, FO 371/52327 (E 884/797/65), PRO.

[36]Telegram 781, Campbell to the Foreign Office, Cairo,
May 3, 1946, FO 371/52520 (E 4026/4/31), PRO; Telegram 205,
Grafftey Smith to the Foreign Office, Jidda, May 26, 1946, FO
371/52526 (E 4833/4/31), PRO.

[37]The Minister in Saudi Arabia (Eddy) to the Secretary of
State, Jidda, May 28, 1946, FRUS, 1946, Vol. VII, pp. 615-616.

[38]Letter, Balfour to Henderson, Washington, June 1, 1946,
FO 371/52528 (E 5406/4/31), PRO.

[39]Telegram 382, Foreign Office to Halifax, London, May 11,
1946, FO 371/52522 (E 42268/4/31), PRO.

[40]Telegram 3020, Attlee to Truman, London, June 10, 1946,
Lot 56D 359, NA.

[41]Telegram 6033, Foreign Office to Inverchapel, London, June
19, 1946, FO 371/52529 (E 5446/4/31), PRO.

[42]The New York Times, June 22, 1946, p. 1; Times (London),
August 13, 1946, p. 4.

[43]Hansard, 415 (1945): 785.

[44]Telegram 3600, Pinkerton to Secretary of State, Jerusalem,
February 25, 1946, 867N.01/2-2546, NA.

[45]Cab. 128/5 CM (46) 1, January 1, 1946, pp. 6-7, PRO.

[46]Ibid. 60, June 20, 1946, pp. 137-139, PRO.

[47]Telegram 6363, Attlee to Truman, London, June 28, 1946, 867N.01/6-2946, NA.

[48]Evan M. Wilson, Decision On Palestine (Stanford: Hoover Institute, 1979), p. 92.

[49]Telegram 6952, Grady to Secretary of State, London, July 24, 1946, 867N.01/72446, NA.

[50]Sir John Balfour, "Diadem Askew; A Diplomatic Cavalcade," Foreign Office Library, London, p. 120.

[51]Nicholas Bethell, The Palestine Triangle (London: Deutsch, pp. 258-264.

[52]Cab. 128/6 CM (46) 72, July 23, 1946, p. 226, PRO.

[53]Telegram 4701, Inverchapel to Foreign Office, Washington, July 23, 1946, FO 371/52543 (E 7007/4/31), PRO.

[54]Wilson, p. 93.

[55]Letter, Hutcheson to McDonald, Houston, August 2, 1946, Papers of James G. McDonald, HHL.

[56]U.S., Congress, Senate, 79th Cong., 2nd sess., Vol. 92, Part 8, July 30, 1946, Congressional Record, p. 10452.

[57]Letter, British Consulate to Embassy in Washington, New York, July 3, 1946, FO 371/52569 (E 6943/4/31), PRO.

[58]Telegram 4862, Inverchapel to Foreign Office, Washington, July 31, 1946, FO 371/52546 (E 7325/4/31), PRO.

[59]Telegram 3744, Harriman to Secretary of State, Paris, July 31, 1946, 867N.01/7-3146, NA.

[60]Telegram 3028, Attlee to Truman, London, August 9, 1946,

Papers of Harry S. Truman, PSF, Foreign Affairs, HSTL.

[61]Cab. 128/6 CM (46), July 26, 1946, p. 219, PRO.

[62]Telegram 335, Grafftey Smith to the Foreign Office, Jidda, August 22, 1946, FO 371/52554 (E 8498/4/31), PRO.

[63]Telegram 741, Young to the Foreign Office, Beirut, August 27, 1946, FO 371/52555 (E 8636/4/31), PRO.

[64]Telegram 1409, Campbell to the Foreign Office, Cairo, August 31, 1946, FO 371/5255 (E 8732/4/31), PRO.

[65]Telegram 1387, Cunningham to the Foreign Office, Palestine, August 27, 1946, FO 371/52555 (E 8615/4/31), PRO.

[66]Memorandum, Clayton to Truman, Washington, September 12, 1946, Papers of Harry S. Truman, PSF, HSTL.

[67]Letter, Inverchapel to Acheson, Washington, October 3, 1946, enclosing copy of a telegram from Attlee to the embassy in Washington, 867N.01/10-346, NA.

[68]Memorandum of a Conversation between Epstein and Henderson, Washington, October 3, 1946, 867N.01/10-346 NA.

[69]Telegram 863, Bevin to the Foreign Office, Paris, October 4, 1946, FO 371/52560 (E 9966/4/31), PRO.

[70]The President to the British Prime Minister (Attlee), Washington, October 10, 1946, FRUS, 1946, Vol. VII, p. 706.

[71]Cab. 128/6 CM (46) 91, October 25, 1946, p. 93, PRO.

[72]Memorandum of a Conversation by the Assistant Secretary of State (Acheson), Washington, November 22, 1946, FRUS, 1946, Vol. VII, pp. 723-725.

[73]Minutes of a Meeting between Jewish Agency Representatives and British Officials, London, October 1, 1946, FO 371/52560

(E 10030/4/31), PRO.

[74]Telegram 2273, Bevin to the Foreign Office, New York, December 4, 1946, FO 371/52646 (E 11893/8035/31), PRO.

[75]Extract from Confidential Notes of Meeting between Truman and Bevin, Washington, December 8, 1946, FO 371/61762 (E 21/46/31), PRO.

[76]Golda Meir, My Life (New York: Dell, 1975), p. 191.

[77]New Palestine, January 17, 1947, p. 2.

[78]Memorandum, Connelly to Truman, Washington, October 2, 1945, PSF, Cabinet, HSTL.

[79]Memorandum, Henderson to Byrnes, Washington, October 9, 1945, Lot 56-D359, NA; Joint Chiefs of Staff to the State-War-Navy Coordinating Committee, Washington, June 21, 1946, FRUS, 1946, Vol. VII, pp. 630-633.

[80]Notes on Meeting with Jewish Agency Representatives, London, January 29, 1947, FO 371/4761873 (E 1074/928/31), PRO.

[81]Cab. 129/17 CP (47) 59, February 13, 1947, p. 60, PRO.

[82]Cab. 128/9 CM (47) 22, February 14, 1947, p. 144, PRO.

NOTES FOR CHAPTER 4

[1]The New York Times, May 15, 1947, p. 1.

[2]Memorandum of a Conversation by the Secretary of State, Washington, June 19, 1947, FRUS, 1947, Vol. V, pp. 1105-1106.

[3]Maurice Richardson, "The Terror Calendar," Observer, May 18, 1947, p. 5.

[4]Zionist Review, June 20, 1947, p. 1.

[5]Quoted in Ibid., June 27, 1947, p. 1.

[6]The New York Times, June 27, 1947, p. 13.

[7]Zionist Review, June 27, 1947, p. 2.

[8]Ibid., July 11, 1947, p. 6.

[9]Jorge Garcia-Granados, The Birth of Israel (New York: Knopf, 1949), pp. 172-173.

[10]Ibid., pp. 208-210.

[11]The New York Times, June 26, 1947, p. 7.

[12]Jacob C. Hurewitz, The Struggle For Palestine (New York: Schocken, 1976), pp. 295-298.

[13]Abba Eban, Abba Ebban, An Autobiography (New York: Random, 1977), p. 70; Loy Henderson, pp. 125-130.

[14]Excerpts from the Minutes of the Sixth Meeting of the United States Delegation to the Second Session of the General Assembly, New York, September 15, 1947, FRUS, 1947, Vol. V, p. 1147; Memorandum prepared in the Department of State, Washington, Ibid., p. 1167.

[15]Telegram 5758, Douglas to the Secretary of State, London, October 28, 1947, Palestine "Reference Book" of Dean Rusk, NA.

[16]The New York Times, November 30, 1947, p. 58.

[17]Quoted in the Times (London), December 1, 1947, p. 4.

[18]Observer, December 21, 1947, p. 5.

[19]Telegram 851, Foreign Office to U.N. Delegation, London, February 23, 1948, FO 371/68648 (E 2628/1078/G), PRO.

[20]Pablo De Azcarate, Mission In Palestine, 1948-1952 (Washington: The Middle East Institute, 1966), p. 14.

[21]Papers of Eben A. Ayers, February 17, 1948, p. 33, HSTL.

[22]Telegram 612, Creech Jones to the Foreign Office, New York, February 21, 1948, FO 371/68648 (E 2628/1078/G), PRO.

[23]Walter Millis (ed.), The Forrestal Diaries (New York: Viking, 1951), p. 387.

[24]Quoted in the New York Times, March 18, 1948, p. 4.

[25]Robert H. Ferrell, The American Secretaries of State And Their Diplomacy Vol. XV George C. Marshall (New York: Cooper Square, 1966), p. 146.

[26]Millis, p. 386.

[27]Papers of Eben A. Ayers, March 20, 1948, HSTL.

[28]Harry S. Truman, The Memoirs of Harry S. Truman Vol. II Years of Trial And Hope (Garden City: Doubleday, 1956), p. 186.

[29]Irwin Ross, The Loneliest Campaign: The Truman Victory Of 1948 (New York: New American Library, 1968), p. 9.

[30]Ibid., pp. 62-63.

[31]Ibid., p. 74.

[32]Telegram 1347, Embassy to Foreign Office, Washington, March 20, 1948, FO 371/68648 (E 3727/1078/G), PRO.

[33]Memorandum, Troutbeck to Foreign Office, Cairo, March 2,

1948, FO 371/68381 (E 3109/681/65), PRO.

[34]Telegram 1292, Foreign Office to U.N. Delegation, London, March 24, 1948, FO 371/48686 (E 3726/1078/G), PRO.

[35]Papers of Eben A. Ayers, March 24, 1948, p. 54, HSTL. For text of Truman's statement see FRUS, 1948, Vol. V, Part 2, pp. 759-760.

[36]Telegram 1469, Embassy to the Foreign Office, Washington, March 26, 1948, FO 371/68648 (E 3914/1078/G), PRO.

NOTES FOR CHAPTER 5

[1]Memorandum, Washington, March 26, 1948, 867N.01/3-2648, NA.

[2]Quoted in Zionist Review, March 26, 1948, p. 2.

[3]Aide Memoire, London, April 13, 1948, FO 371/68649 (E 4790/ 1078/31), PRO.

[4]The Acting Secretary of State to the Embassy in the United Kingdom, Washington, April 17, 1948, FRUS, 1948, Vol. V, Part 2, pp. 828-824; The American Ambassador in the United Kingdom to the Secretary of State, London, April 20, 1948, Ibid., p. 837.

[5]Sir Alex Kirkbride, A Crackle of Thorns (London: Murray, 1956), pp. 157-158.

[6]Quoted in Zionist Review, April 30, 1948, p. 4.

[7]Record of a Conversation between Attlee, Bevin, and Douglas, London, April 28, 1948, FO 371/68649 (E 5751/1078/G), PRO.

[8]Memorandum of a Conversation between Henderson and Beeley, Washington, May 2, 1948, 867N.01/5-1248, NA.

[9]Papers of Eben A. Ayers, May 8, 1948, pp. 92-93, HSTL.

[10]Telegram 2077, Douglas to Secretary of State, London, May 12, 1948, 867N.01/5-1248, NA.

[11]The New York Times, May 12, 1948, p. 16.

[12]Truman, p. 164.

[13]Memorandum of a Conversation by the Undersecretary of State (Lovett), Washington, May 21, 1948, FRUS, 1948, Vol. V, Part 2, pp. 119-120.

[14]The Ambassador in the United Kingdom (Douglas) to the

Secretary of State, London, June 19, 1948, Ibid., pp. 1124-1125.
[15]The Secretary of State (Marshall) to the Ambassador in
the United Kingdom, June 25, 1948, Ibid., pp. 1148-1149.

[16]Memorandum of a Conversation by the Undersecretary of
State (Lovett), Washington, August 26, 1948, Ibid., pp. 1345-1347.

[17]Sir John Glubb, A Soldier With The Arabs (New York:
Harpers, 1957), pp. 99-120.

[18]Zionist Review, June 25, 1948, p. 2.

[19]Telegram 426, Meyer to Secretary of State, Baghdad, July
6, 1948, "Palestine Reference Book" of Dean Rusk, NA.

[20]Telegram 3055, Douglas to Secretary of State, London,
July 8, 1948, McClintock Palestine File, NA.

[21]Telegram 3909, Douglas to Secretary of State, London,
August 30, 1948, "Palestine Reference Book" of Dean Rusk, NA.

[22]Memorandum of a Conversation, New York, June 12, 1948,
"Palestine Reference Book" of Dean Rusk, NA.

[23]Memorandum, McClintock to Ethridge, Washington, January
28, 1949, Ibid.

[24]Letter, McClintock to Rusk, Washington, July 1, 1948,
Ibid.; it is interesting that speaking at a session of the
American Historical Association in Washington on December 28,
1976, the historian Howard M. Sachar said that Rusk anticipated
a weekend at Martha's Vineyard where he could "wash the sins of
the chosen people off my back." The Palestine Question in
American History (New York: Arno, 1978), p. 112.

[25]Memorandum, Marshall to Truman, Washington, August 16,

1948, Papers of Harry S. Truman, PSF, HSTL.

[26]Telegram 3606, Douglas to the Secretary of State, September 1, 1948, London, "Palestine Reference Book" of Dean Rusk, NA.

[27]Telegram 3583, Marshall to embassy in London, Washington, September 10, 1948, Ibid.

[28]Telegram 3802, Douglas to Secretary of State, London, September 12, 1948, Ibid.

[29]Progress Report of the U.N. Mediator On Palestine Rhodes, September 16, 1948 (London: HMSO, 1948).

[30]The New York Times.

[31]Eban, p. 132.

[32]John Snetsinger, Truman, The Jewish Vote And The Creation of Israel (Stanford: Hoover Institute, 1974), p. 125.

[33]Eban, p. 134.

[34]Snetsinger, pp. 129-131.

[35]Letter, Lewis Jones to McClintock, London, November 16, 1948, "Palestine Reference Book" of Dean Rusk, NA.

[36]Message, Bevin to Marshall, Washington, November 23, 1948, Ibid.

[37]David Ben-Gurion, Israel: A Personal History (New York: Funk & Wagnalls, 1971), p. 277.

[38]Memorandum, McClintock to Ethridge, Washington, January 28, 1949, "Palestine Reference Book" of Dean Rusk, NA.

[39]Telegram 1528, Burdett to Secretary of State, Jerusalem, December 11, 1948, Ibid.

NOTES FOR CHAPTER 6

[1]James Morris, The Hashemite Kings (New York: Pantheon,
1959), p. 100.

[2]Letter, Kirkbride to Foreign Office, Amman, September 24,
1946, FO 371/10091 (E 5507/80), PRO.

[3]Ibid., October 10, 1947, FO 371/99181 (E 653/80), PRO.

[4]Telegram 321, Ibid., October 29, 1947, FO 371/10711 (E
3765/80), PRO.

[5]Telegram 2081, Douglas to the Secretary of State, London,
May 12, 1948, "Palestine Reference Book" of Dean Rusk, NA.

[6]Sir Alec Kirkbride, From the Wings: Amman Memoirs 1947-
1951 (London: Cass, 1976), p. 29.

[7]Telegram 43, Kirkbride to Foreign Office, Amman, August 6,
1948, FO 371/10720 (E 20/11/80), PRO.

[8]Telegram 361, BMEO to Foreign Office, Cairo, September 17,
1948, FO 371/12 (E 23/375/31), PRO.

[9]Telegram 753, Kirkbride to Foreign Office, Amman, September
25, 1948, FO 371/2502 (E 375/31), PRO.

[10]Telegram 1589, Foreign Office to Cairo, London, September
19, 1948, FO 371/1809 (E 11675/80G), PRO.

[11]Telegram 1315, Andrews to Foreign Office, Cairo, September
20, 1948, FO 371 (E 12277/1165/80G), PRO.

[12]Letter, Glubb to Burrows, Amman, September 22, 1948, FO
371/2651 (E 11675/80G), PRO.

[13]Telegram 386, BMEO to Foreign Office, Cairo, October 4,
1948, FO 371 (E 12907/1165/80G), PRO.

[14]Telegram 544, Bergus to Secretary of State, Jidda, October 5, 1948, "Palestine Reference Book" of Dean Rusk, NA.

[15]Telegram 64, Stabler to Secretary of State, Amman, September 25, 1948, McClintock Palestine File, NA.

[16]Telegram 77, Ibid., October 9, 1948, Ibid.

[17]Telegram 76, Ibid., October 8, 1948, Ibid.

[18]Letter, Embassy to Foreign Office, Washington, July 15, 1946, FO 371 (E 6948/5507/80), PRO.

[19]Telegram, Lord Inverchapel to Foreign Office, Washington, June 17, 1946, FO 371 (E 5507/5507/180), PRO.

[20]Telegram 862, Burdett to Secretary of State, Jerusalem, June 7, 1948, "Palestine Reference Book" of Dean Rusk, NA.

[21]Telegram 2401, Douglas to Secretary of State, London, June 1, 1948, McClintock Palestine File, NA.

[22]Telegram 933, Burdett to Secretary of State, Jerusalem, June 17, 1948, Ibid.

[23]Telegram 3470, Marshall to Douglas, Washington, September 1, 1948, "Palestine Reference Book" of Dean Rusk, NA.

[24]Memorandum of a Conversation, London, August 20, 1948, FO 371 (E 11373/6090/31), PRO.

[25]Telegram 213, Franks to Foreign Office, Washington, January 11, 1949, FO 371 (AN 135/1023/45G), PRO.

[26]Cab. 128/15 CM (49) 3, January 17, 1949, p. 16, PRO.

[27]Cab. 128/15 CM (49) 6, January 24, 1949, p. 26, PRO.

[28]Telegram 325, Holmes to Secretary of State, London, 501. BB Palestine 1-2649, NA.

[29]Letter, Jones to Satterthwaite, London, February 2, 1949,

501. BB Palestine 2-249.

[30]Meir, pp. 206-211.

[31]Telegram 4627, Douglas to Secretary of State, London, September 20, 1948, "Palestine Reference Book" of Dean Rusk, NA.

[32]Telegram 4829, Ibid., November 11, 1948, Ibid.

[33]Telegram 252, McDonald to Secretary of State, Tel Aviv, November 11, 1948, Ibid.

[34]Telegram 942, Kirkbride to Foreign Office, Amman, December 9, 1948, FO 371 (E 15724/11675/80G), PRO.

[35]Telegram 15243, Douglas to Secretary of State, London, December 14, 1948, McClintock Palestine File, NA.

[36]Ruth Dayan and Helga Dudman, And Perhaps: The Story of Ruth Dayan (New York: Harcourt Brace Jovanovich, 1973), p. 123.

[37]Telegram 54, Stabler to Secretary of State, Amman, February 8, 1949, "Palestine Reference Book" of Dean Rusk, NA.

[38]Telegram 61, Ibid., February 16, 1949, Ibid.

[39]Telegram 66, Ibid., February 16, 1949, Ibid.

[40]Telegram 74, Stabler to Secretary of State, Amman, February 26, 1949, "Palestine Reference Book" of Dean Rusk, NA.

[41]Telegram 145, Acheson to Tel Aviv, Washington, March 9, 1949, Ibid.

[42]Telegram, McDonald to Secretary of State, Tel Aviv, March 11, 1949, 867N.01/3-1149, NA.

[43]Telegram 964, Stabler to Secretary of State, Amman, March 14, 1949, "Palestine Reference Book" of Dean Rusk, NA.

[44]Telegram 116, Ibid., March 17, 1949, Ibid.

[45]Telegram 1051, Douglas to Secretary of State, London,

March 18, 1949, Ibid.

[46] Telegram 1202, Ibid., March 25, 1949, Ibid.

[47] Moshe Dayan, Story of My Life (New York: Warner, 1977), pp. 176-177.

[48] Telegram A-17, Stabler to Secretary of State, Amman, April 3, 1949, 867N.01/4-349, NA.

[49] Dayan, p. 171.

[50] Telegram 274, McDonald to Secretary of State, Tel Aviv, April 12, 1949, "Palestine Reference Book" of Dean Rusk, NA.

[51] The New York Times, April 8, 1949, p. 9.

[52] Sir John Bagot Glubb, A Soldier With The Arabs (New York: Harper, 1957), p. 241.

[53] Telegram 165, Stabler to Secretary of State, April 15, 1949, 867N.01/4-1549, NA.

[54] Telegram 62, Acheson to Legation in Jidda, Washington, February 19, 1949, "Palestine Reference Book" of Dean Rusk, NA.

[55] Telegram 79, Stabler to Secretary of State, Amman, March 2, 1949, Ibid.

[56] Letter, Troutbeck to Wright, Cairo, March 3, 1949, FO 371 (E 158/1052/65), PRO.

[57] Letter, Dow to Foreign Office, Jerusalem, March 15, 1949, FO 371 (E 3763/1052/65), PRO.

[58] Telegram 70, Pirie Gordon to Foreign Office, Amman, August 15, 1949, FO 371 (E 10169/1013/80), PRO.

[59] Kirkbride, p. 36.

[60] Telegram 174, Bevin to Pirie Gordon, London, August 22, 1949, FO 371 (E 10299/1055/80), PRO.

[61]Telegram 4375, Franks to Foreign Office, Washington, September 14, 1949, FO 371 (E 1158/10811/809), PRO.

[62]Telegram 806, Foreign Office to Amman, London, October 20, 1949, FO 371 (E 12317/1025/80), PRO.

[63]Telegram 80, Kirkbride to Foreign Office, October 31, 1949, FO 371 (E 13468/1025/80), PRO.

[64]Telegram 50, Ibid., April 15, 1950, FO (ET 1081/6), PRO.

[65]Telegram 125, Dow to Foreign Office, Jerusalem, April 26, 1950, FO 371 (ET 1081/21), PRO.

[66]Telegram 176, Stabler to Secretary of State, Amman, December 29, 1948, "Palestine Reference Book" of Dean Rusk, NA.

[67]Telegram 1263, Franks to Foreign Office, Washington, April 24, 1950, FO 371 (ET 1081/5), PRO.

[68]Letter, Kirkbride to Furlonge, Amman, May 25, 1950, FO 371 (ET 1081/67), PRO.

[69]Telegram 161, Kirkbride to Foreign Office, Amman, April 25, 1950, FO 371 (ET 1081/23), PRO.

[70]Telegram 190, Helm to Foreign Office, Tel Aviv, April 25, 1950, FO 371 (ET 1081/18), PRO.

[71]Telegram 126, Troutbeck to Foreign Office, Cairo, May 5, 1950, FO 371 (ET 1081/57), PRO.

[72]Telegram 1346, Foreign Office to Baghdad, May 25, 1950, FO 371 (E 1071/61), PRO.

[73]Letter, McMan to Furlonge, Damascus, May 29, 1950, FO 371 (E 1071/75), PRO.

[74]Telegram 209, Kirkbride to Foreign Office, Amman, May 30, 1950, FO 371 (E 1071/701), PRO.

[75]Letter, Kirkbride to Furlonge, Amman, May 22, 1950, FO 371 (E 107/174), PRO.

[1]Michael Bar-Zohar, Ben-Gurion A Biography (New York: Delacorte Press, 1977), pp. 153-154.

[2]Minute by Helm, London, March 25, 1949, FO 371 (E 4307/ 1051/31), PRO.

[3]Minute by Beith, London, March 29, 1949, FO 371 (E 4691/ 1052/65), PRO.

[4]Telegram 2174, Foreign Office to Washington, London, April 13, 1949, FO 371 (E 4779/1054/131), PRO.

[5]Telegram 3, Helm to Foreign Office, Tel Aviv, May 23, 1949, FO 371 (E 6561/1054/131), PRO.

[6]Letter, Helm to Bevin, Tel Aviv, June 15, 1949, FO 371 (E 7920/151/131/G), PRO.

[7]Telegram 206, Helm to Foreign Office, Tel Aviv, July 26, 1949, FO 371 (E 8696/1054/131), PRO.

[8]Minute by Burrows, London, December 7, 1949, FO 371 (E 15164/1056/131), PRO.

[9]Letter, Helm to Strang, Tel Aviv, April 11, 1950, FO 371 (EE 1017/30), PRO.

[10]Telegram 318, Foreign Office to Tel Aviv, London, April 26, 1950, FO 371 (E 1053/9), PRO.

[11]Memorandum of a Conversation by Assistant Secretary of State for Near Eastern Affairs, Washington, January 11, 1950, FRUS, 1950, Vol. V, pp. 680-681.

[12]Telegram 256, Franks to Foreign Office, Washington, January 21, 1950, FO 371 (EE 1015/9), PRO.

[13]Telegram 428, Hoyar Millart to Foreign Office, Washington, February 6, 1950, FO 371 (EE 1015/18), PRO.

[14]Telegram 75, Kirkbride to Foreign Office, Amman, February 18, 1950, FO 371 (E 1015/27), PRO.

[15]Telegram 185, Helm to Foreign Office, Tel Aviv, February 27, 1950, FO 371 (EE 1015/32), PRO.

[16]Telegram, Kirkbride to Foreign Office, Amman, February 20, 1950, FO 371 (EE 1015/28), PRO.

[17]Telegram 90, Strang to Foreign Office, Ankara, March 11, 1950, FO 371 (ET 1024/6), PRO.

[18]Telegram 144, Foreign Office to Washington, London, March 16, 1950, FO 371 (ET 1024/8), PRO.

[19]Letter, Helm to Furlonge, Tel Aviv, March 10, 1950, FO 371 (ET 1024/19), PRO.

[20]Letter, Furlonge to Helm, London, March 23, 1950 (ET 1024/9), PRO.

[21]The Ambassador in Israel (McDonald) to the Secretary of State, Tel Aviv, March 6, 1950, FRUS, 1950, Vol. V, p. 782.

[22]Memorandum of a Conversation by the Secretary of State, Washington, March 9, 1950, Ibid., pp. 788-789.

[23]Letter, Helm to Wright, Tel Aviv, February 14, 1950, FO 371 (E 1015/31), PRO.

[24]Ibid., October 15, 1950, FO 371 (ER 1905/3/G), PRO.

[25]Ibid., February 14, 1950, FO 371 (1015/31), PRO.

[26]Telegram 161, Kirkbride to Foreign Office, Amman, April 25, 1950, FO 371 (ET 1081/23), PRO.

[27]The New York Times, April 24, 1950, p. 10.

[28]*New Palestine*, May 1950, p. 1.

[29]Telegram 398, Campbell to Foreign Office, Cairo, May 6, 1950, FO 371 (E 1071/42), PRO.

[30]The *New York Times*, May 7, 1950, p. 1.

[31]Ibid., May 10, 1950, p. 3.

[32]Letter, Kirkbride to Furlonge, Amman, July 14, 1950, FO 371 (EE 1015/77), PRO.

[33]Minute by Davies, London, September 15, 1950, FO 371 (ER 1054/47), PRO.

[34]Eban, pp. 155-156.

[35]Telegram 348, Kirkbride to Foreign Office, Amman, October 13, 1950, FO 371 (EE 1015/103), PRO.

[36]Minute by Furlonge, London, October 20, 1950, FO 371 (EE 1015/107), PRO.

[37]Letter, Helm to Wright, Tel Aviv, November 11, 1950, FO 371 (E 1031/193/50), PRO.

[38]Telegram 12, Kirkbride to Foreign Office, Amman, December 18, 1950, FO 371 (EE 1091/248), PRO.

[39]Quoted in Gaddis Smith, *The American Secretaries of State And Their Diplomacy* Vol. XVI *Dean Acheson* (New York: Cooper Square, 1972), p. 247.

A study of the problem of Anglo-American relations and
Palestine during the years 1945-1950 necessitates research in
both American and British archives. A primary source of
information is the National Archives in Washington, D.C., where
in the Diplomatic Records of the State Department file 867N.01
provides insight into formation of Palestine policy and
correspondence between Washington and London that underlines the
complexity of Anglo-American diplomacy. Considerable material
from this file has been published in Foreign Relations of the
United States but in some cases comments that give insight into
the opinions of State Department policy-makers have been omitted.
Other important sources at the National Archives are the files of
two officials who dealt with the Palestine problem, Dean Rusk and
Robert McClintock; although these files contain considerable
duplication both are necessary for an understanding of the
problem.

The Harry S. Truman Library in Independence, Missouri, is a
storehouse of material. Among the valuable sources is the Diary
of Eben A. Ayers containing daily accounts of meetings that the
president held with top officials to discuss party politics as
well as national policy. Other important sources are the Papers
of Harry S. Truman, the President's Secretary's File, the Papers
of Samuel I. Rosenman, the Papers of Clark Clifford, and an oral
history interview with Loy Henderson that provides insight into
the attitude of a career foreign service officer with

considerable experience in the Middle East.

Another excellent site for research is the Herbert H. Lehman Library at Columbia University in New York City, location of the Papers of James G. McDonald from his appointment to the Anglo-American Committee of Inquiry in 1945 until his return to the United States from his post as first ambassador to Israel in 1950. New York City is also the location of the Zionist Archives housing an outstanding collection of periodicals published by the Zionist organizations both in Britain and the United States. Although some issues are missing it is possible to chronicle daily life in Palestine--Israel after 1948--and to document the Zionist position. The most useful publications are the New Palestine and Zionist Review.

In Britain the Public Records Office in Kew is the major repository of records dealing with the British role in Palestine. The records in Kew are well organized and there is no duplication of telegrams and memoranda as is the case in Washington. Each year newly released files are arranged by Foreign Office Department and then by country. Most useful documents are in the Middle Eastern Department index under Palestine, Israel, and Transjordan. The file number for these documents is FO 371 (Political Correspondence), and these files may be ordered by computer. In addition the Cabinet Papers (Cab. 128) and Cabinet Memoranda (Cab. 129) are available in the reading room; these papers make it possible to study policy making at the highest level and underline the role of Foreign Secretary Bevin.

The most useful published records are Foreign Relations of

the United States Palestine volumes 1945-1950, the Congressional
Record 1945-1950 and Hansard's Parliamentary Debates (Commons)
1945-1950. Also helpful are Public Papers of the Presidents of
the United States: Harry S. Truman, 1945-1950.

Numerous diaries, reminiscences, biographies, and
autobiographies have been written by and about those who
participated in trying to find a solution for the Palestine
problem. For an account of early Zionist efforts to involve the
American government in this matter see: David W. Levy and Melvin
I. Urofsky (eds.), Letters of Louis D. Brandeis Vol. IV (Albany,
1975), and for an account of American Jewish reluctance to get
involved with Zionism in the years immediately after World War I
see: Cyrus Adler, Jacob H. Schiff: His Life And Letters Vol. II
(Garden City, 1929). For an account of Britain's early years in
Palestine when it seemed that perhaps the British government
might be successful see: John Bowle, Viscount Samuel (London,
1957). For an eloquent account of the Zionist struggle to
achieve a state see: Chaim Weizmann, Trial and Error (New York,
1973). Some of the leading Anglo-American statesmen wrote to
justify their positions, and often omitted any real examination
of their policies. The interesting books in this category are:
Harry S. Truman, Memoirs of Harry S. Truman 1946-1952: Years of
Trial and Hope (Garden City, 1956), and two books by Francis
Williams, A Prime Minister Remembers; The War and PostWar Memoirs
of Earl Attlee (London, 1961), and Ernest Bevin, Portrait of a
Great Englishman (London, 1952). Two members of the Anglo-
American Committee of Inquiry, one Briton and one American, wrote

accounts of the investigation. Both became Zionists and their books reflect their sympathy for the Jews. See: Bartley C. Crum, Behind the Silken Curtain (New York, 1947) and Richard Crossman, Palestine Mission (New York, 1947). An important source of information about King Abdullah and the special relationship between Britain and Jordan is: Alec Kirkbride, From the Wings; Amman Memoirs, 1947-1951 (London, 1976). An account of Jordan's role in Palestine can be found in: Sir John Glubb, A Soldier with the Arabs (New York, 1957). The Israeli view can be found in Abba Eban, An Autobiography (New York, 1977) and in David Ben-Gurion, A Personal History (Tel Aviv, 1971). The experience of a pro-Zionist member of UNSCOP is related in Jorge Garcia-Granados, The Birth of Israel (New York, 1949), and the difficulties of a U.N. employee in Palestine are explained by Pablo De Azcarate in Mission in Palestine, 1948-1952 (Washington, 1966).

An excellent study of the relationship between the United States and the Jewish state is Israel in the Mind of America by Peter Grose (New York, 1983). Two books that deal with American politics and the Palestine question, both published by the Hoover Institute are: John Snetsinger, Truman, the Jewish Vote and the Creation of Israel (Stanford, 1974) and Evan M. Wilson, Decision on Palestine (Stanford, 1979). Snetsinger's book is short on analysis while Wilson's book, written after thirty years in the Foreign Service, reflects his personal experience dealing with the Palestine problem. Another book on the same subject is Zvi Ganin, Truman, American Jewry, and Israel, 1945-1948 (New York,

1979).

Michael Cohen in Retreat From the Mandate: The Making of British Policy, 1936-1945 (New York, 1978) expertly presents the background for British postwar policy, and in Palestine and the Great Powers (Princeton, 1982), discusses that policy. Nicholas Bethell in The Palestine Triangle (London, 1979) superbly documents Britain's role in Palestine from 1935-1948. An early book that is useful for an understanding of Britain's policy is Elizabeth Monroe, Britain's Moment in the Middle East, 1914-1956 (Baltimore, 1963).

Two books, originally published before the availability of most of the documents that remain excellent sources for an understanding of the Palestine problem are: J. C. Hurewitz, The Struggle for Palestine (New York, 1950), and Christopher Sykes, Crossroads to Israel (London, 1965); both books have been reissued, the former in 1976 and the latter in 1973.

The Palestine problem received considerable coverage in the press and many periodicals devoted much space to the matter. The New York Times and the Times (London) presented news from Palestine daily and Time magazine gave its readers a weekly report. Commentary, Atlantic, and Harper's published perceptive articles and scholarly journals analyzed the dilemma. Some of the best articles can be found in the Journal of Middle East Studies and in Middle Eastern Studies.

Ralph F. de Bedts

AMBASSADOR JOSEPH KENNEDY 1938–1940

An Anatomy of Appeasement

American University Studies: Series IX, History. Vol. 12
ISBN 0-8204-0229-X   280 pp.   hardcover/lam. US $ 31.15
recommended prices – alterations reserved

Joe Kennedy, in return for his extensive support for President Franklin Roosevelt, became the first Irish-American and the first Catholic to attain the highest US diplomatic post: Ambassador to Great Britain's Court of St. James. But his complete lack of knowledge of Hitler and Nazism and his devotion to international trade led him to a staunch appeasement which lasted even longer than did Chamberlain's. His reports and ambassadorial conversations became increasingly distorted by his appeasement bias. Recalled when his defeatist remarks were no longer tolerable in a Britain under enemy siege, he continued his appeasement and isolationist speeches in the US until the outbreak of war.

Contents: Joseph Kennedy, the individualistic stock market specialist whom Roosevelt posted to Great Britain's Court of St. James, pushed his appeasement and defeatist line so brashly that a Presidential recall was necessary.

PETER LANG PUBLISHING, INC.
62 West 45th Street
USA – New York, NY 10036